# UNBOUND
# 100 DAYS
# *of* INTENT

# SHERRI M. DAY

# UNBOUND
# 100 DAYS
# *of* INTENT

## A Memoir and Trauma
## Healing Journal

gatekeeper press™

Columbus, Ohio

Unbound 100 Days of Intent: A Memoir and Trauma Healing Journal

Published by Gatekeeper Press
2167 Stringtown Rd, Suite 109
Columbus, OH 43123-2989
www.GatekeeperPress.com

Library of Congress Control Number: 2020947739

ISBN (paperback): 9781662905582
eISBN: 9781662905599

*May We Never Abandon Ourselves Again.*

*"Rex" and "M,"*
*I See You. I Hear You.*
*Thank you for seeing my heart. Thank you for hearing my voice.*
*Thank you for encouraging me to share my story.*

*I grew with love because of you.*
*S*

*"How do I release all this rage? The pain inside?" I asked her.
"Set your intent," she replied with casual calmness.*

*What the fuck, I thought. Set my intent. For what?
I just want to feel again.*

*~ Sher Unbound*

# Contents

# From the Author

*"Our Inner Child knows the truth.*
*Let them speak to us now."*
*~Sher Unbound*

*I honor your courage for reaching this far. Far enough to want to survive. Far enough to want to take any step necessary or possible to take a deeper breath, sleep a little easier, release a little more of the shame you've held onto and continued to embody. Shame which was not and is not yours to hold.*

*This next question is symbolic of extending my hand to you, so that we may dive below the surface together. What was the worst lie you told as a kid? Anytime in your life? Mine was lying to myself, as recently as during the editing process of this book. While editing, the realization came to me of all the numerous stories I had told myself for years. Page after page of stories, void of so much that I was omitting, and writing it all off as insignificant to the reader.*

*But it's significant to me. This was my life; I lived and survived these days. The act of omitting these stories was not only negating my experience, but it also removed my feelings. Furthering the power, I continued to allow the shameful situations to take from me, keeping my heart bound. After coming to this realization and owning the minimizing of myself, I made the brave choice to breathe life to my feelings.*

*Finally, there is validation of my essence as a human being, and rightfully so. I am here, and I fought hard to take my place here, even when it felt like there was no progress; sometimes leaving a feeling of hopelessness. I am still here (and I am grateful you are too).*

*How will anyone ever know the reason for my existence if I don't tell what was happening inside – what I experienced as a child? How will anyone ever know they are not alone if my voice is silent and if I believe I have nothing of value to share? How can I release the shame that belonged to my abusers – the shame that wasn't mine to carry in the first place?*

*Under the threat of punishment, instructions were engraved on my soul to never tell about the "special love." In efforts to survive, beginning at my earliest recollections at the age of three, I adapted and conformed.*

*Omitting my feelings about all the years of abuse and abandonment was one of the worst offenses committed in my life. Living for more than three-fourths of my life without acknowledging the truth of all that I felt, it took more than an emotional toll on me. Life was challenged by enduring mental, physical, and emotional illnesses created from holding shame. Without realizing it, I was creating a life of self-abuse; repeating abusive relationships and spiraling into severe behavioral/emotional dysfunction to avoid the pain of my past.*

*But... the only way out is through. The day arrived when there was no choice but to finally give myself permission to allow the feelings to pass. Through this process, I learned an extremely vital lesson. The feelings we fear and hide from, they are only temporary. Those nasty, painful feelings are only TEMPORARY. Personal experience taught me while working through intense inner work in Myles Scott's eight-week group program and personal coaching; countless hours of inner work, journaling, and long intense talks with my soul sister, Christina "Rex" Fedorchenko; intense inner work with*

*The Way of Impeccability Program by Syl Sebastian and reading that those feelings are only perceptions based in fear. My choice was to go through the feelings or ignore them as I had been doing all my life.*

*One would think after a year of intense inner work (that is an understatement), a person would be able to freely express their feelings. But still, I could not. I knew something deeply personal had to be done just for me, by me, to train myself to feel. The idea came like a jolt to my system because of the simplicity: Set my Intent.*

*The title, "Unbound – 100 Days of Intent" reflects just that: 100 days of setting my intention to feel, unbind, unlock, and unleash the feelings deliberately hidden for most of my life. Each day editing and rewriting this journal uncovered more feelings, and finally the feelings began to flow, permeating the pages. Days of writing and rewriting until I was fully satisfied with my feelings; they were raw and real, and I felt every word I had written.*

*To provide further context to that story, a few months ago I was struggling with the purpose of authoring my story. Other than my own catharsis in telling it, who would really care to read it, and what would they do with it? There was a nagging feeling that remained: there was some message to the madness I had survived. I was determined to find out what that was.*

*After speaking at length to my soul sister and best friend, Rex, on this question, she suggested I simply sit with it. I spoke my intention of wanting to know what my purpose was, and she reminded me the work had been done; now was the time to trust the process. Grudgingly, I put the thoughts away with a bit of effort and forgot about the need to know what my life purpose was/is. She is good at reminding me to set my intent and appreciate my value.*

*Then, as casual conversation and "aha" moments go, my purpose presented itself. In another conversation on the need to express my feelings, a redirection of this book and my purpose was right there – as casual and natural as the breath I take.*

*To reach my inner child and give her the love I knew we both needed, 100 days would be spent going over every word, each line, each story, and applying my feelings to each. My book suddenly took on a purpose, with an identity of its own – just as I now know who I am.*

*Then, it happened. Working with further edits, I sat back and reread a letter. What was I doing? I was aware of the "why" behind sharing my story, but there was an important point missing. The story was being written from a point of view that was not conducive to healing for anyone reading my story. The writing was being shared by the voice of a victim.*

*There is a process of sharing our stories as survivors of sexual assault. To heal, we share our stories with feeling and authenticity until we reach the point of acceptance, compassion, and understanding. This point is not in question with survivors. There were two questions I needed to answer to continue sharing with the hope of reaching others: What is my responsibility when sharing my story? And what is my intention in sharing it?*

*My intent is healing for others through love. Love is the only truth.*

*The only time we spend as a victim is during any part of the abuse as it occurred. When the abuse ends, we are survivors. I became a woman who struggled to find a way to live with the perceptions of the feelings absorbed through the abuser's actions. What does all this mean? I survived but lived as a victim. Victims blame, struggle, and crave love.*

*While authoring the story, I was actively releasing the shame I carried and lived in as though it were mine. During editing, and today especially, there was a shift in my heart and consciousness. How can I share the love and the message that you can heal your inner child wounds if all I am giving you are the details you already have lived through yourself?*

*Here is where it gets tricky if you are not ready to understand. My story is being written and shared with the love it deserves. My abusers deserve to be understood with compassion offered through love and forgiveness.*

*If I am telling the world I am healing and that the only real thing is love, then my responsibility is to heal with love – and share that healing process with you as co-survivors.*

*My energy shifted from one of a survivor to a full understanding of the meanings of "transcendent" and "creator." I cannot, in good conscience, write from the space of my old self. That part of me is forever gone, and all that remains is the truth of love. My energy needs to come from love, compassion, and understanding.*

*What is a survivor's responsibility in sharing their story? Talk about the ugly parts first. Pour them out and let them go. As hard as it may seem, tell it from your heart space with love. In the end, that's all there is – the truth of love.*

*I invite you to set your intent for whatever healing you need on your journey toward self-discovery after trauma and write deeply. Take your time, feel every feeling that comes, and let it through. I encourage you to read your writing back to yourself and ask if you are being deeply honest with yourself. Is this what you felt? Take note if you are hitting any blocks. There is more packed behind that block. Unbelievably, within that block lies gold. I encourage you to lean in, go there. Take your time but go there.*

*There is something cathartic about expressing yourself through writing that I have not found in the best of therapists. This journal can be used as a tool to assist you with the release of shame, guilt, and/or other emotions that prevent us from achieving what we desire most: Self-love.*

*We all have the answers we seek inside. I hope you find your answers within your writing.*

*Before you begin, here are a few notes on how to use this journal.*

*Grab a cup of tea or coffee. Get yourself comfortable and settle in for this. Take your time reading each story, responding as you feel called. The bold text is your journaling prompt, but you are free to write as you are moved by any part of the story. I am merely extending my story to you in this journal form in hopes that you can use it as a tool along your own journey.*

*It is recommended that you purchase a comfortable writing tablet(s) and a few good pens. Hand-writing your journal is important, as it slows down the process of thought and prevents you from editing as you write, allowing for the free flow of thoughts and emotions. This allows you to process what you are feeling in the moment.*

*As you write, start on the surface, taking note of the feelings arising in your body. Ask yourself, "What am I feeling right now?" and begin to process your feelings by writing, "I Feel" and then completing the sentence/thoughts. Write again, asking yourself why you feel this way. What is coming up for you at this moment? What is this feeling reminiscent of? For example, "I fear being rejected." Answer that with why you feel that way. Take note of any memories that may come up around this feeling as well. Repeat.*

*During this process, be gentle with yourself. You did not choose the trauma, but you are making a choice to show up for yourself in this moment and can choose to heal. Extend grace, understanding, and patience to yourself. It is common for this process to take about seven passes of writing as you uncover layer after layer before discovering exactly why you feel the feeling you are experiencing. Once you do, you have arrived at the root (underlying cause) of the fear or block.*

*Write as much as you need to. Revisit prompts or parts of the story as many times as necessary until you have uncovered any remaining blocks. I encourage you to lean all the way into the blocks that you encounter that leave you feeling certain there is nothing there. You may find yourself feeling nothing, seeing nothing at all, hearing yourself saying, "I do not remember anything," and quickly shrugging off this time; dig further. Right there within this block is some major gold, I promise you. But don't take my word for it. Please, find the treasure yourself.*

*Use the prompts as inspiration for your own questions. Asking questions is a good way to arrive at how and why we feel the way we do.*

*Although this is my story, this journal is for you. Each page is a small snapshot of a significant moment in my life, shared in the hopes that some part of it will resonate with you, and in turn, help to illuminate your path.*

*There is a lot to absorb and digest here. If you feel it's too much, don't push yourself to write. Take a break, meditate, take a walk, or do any other grounding technique you use and come back with renewed thoughts to author your story.*

*If you need assistance or would like to work with me in furthering your life journey, you can write to me at sherunbound@gmail.com or find me on Instagram @sher_unbound.*

# Foreword

The path of healing for many people, including myself, comes at the point of reaching their emotional threshold. When the pain of staying the same becomes greater than the anticipated pain of change, you have two options: kill yourself or attempt to claw your way out of the dark abyss. At the time Sher was starting her healing journey, she had just hit her emotional threshold and found a glimmer of hope after joining an online community of mine that provided a safe space to show up as your authentic self.

"Be kind to everyone because you don't know what they're going through," is a quote I try to live by, and it certainly feels like an understatement as it applies to Sher. When I met her online, I wasn't aware that she had recently attempted to end her life. If she had told me why at the time, I wouldn't have been able to fathom the depth of her pain, even though I too have a history of depression and suicidal ideation. Although we've grown close over time, both as friends and in a professional capacity, there is no amount of time spent, words shared, or deep-healing coaching sessions that could possibly allow me to fully understand what it's like to walk a day in her shoes.

How could I comprehend what she's been through? Should I take her on as a client? Would I be able to help her? These were all thoughts I had when Sher asked over a video call for private coaching sessions. Despite my reservations, there was something special about her that I couldn't overlook.

The greatest factor of a client's success is their willingness to learn and apply what is shared. Ever since that glimmer of hope, Sher has proved that her will is indomitable. When she sets her mind to a task, you can bet it will be completed no matter the obstacle. I've never met someone who sponges information quite like her. She doesn't miss any details, she questions everything, and she thinks ideas and concepts all the way through to the end. She never gets complacent, and although the inner work can often be frustrating and uncomfortable, she never gives up. The first assignment I ever gave her was to make vulnerable journal entries to unlock the subconscious mind and gain access to repressed emotions. Little did I know that almost a year later, those journal entries would form the basis of this very book.

This is the story of a woman whose journey is nothing short of awe-inspiring. To face her past, she had to take the plunge into the most painful places trapped in the recesses of her mind. She had buried a lifetime of trauma deep within her subconscious mind and her nervous system to detach from tremendous levels of shame, guilt, and resentment, which resulted in emotional numbness and the loss of specific memories among other things.

Over the past year, I've been privileged to witness Sher grow in the best of ways. Despite the challenges she has faced, both in her earlier life and now, she has prevailed. She chooses to show up for herself after a lifetime of believing her sole purpose in life was to please others. She has returned home to herself after compassionately releasing decades of compounded shame, guilt, and resentment. And now she is courageous enough to share her most vulnerable truths with you.

There is hardly a greater honor for me than to have contributed, in some small way, to the inspiring and empowering story of a woman who has overcome inconceivable challenges in her life. May we all learn to face our demons with as much courage as Sher.

With love, Myles Scott

*A power-surge. That's how it felt. Waking up to a slow-moving electric buzz in my body, recognizing it first in my legs, warming throughout my body. It wasn't sudden; this was a gradual movement – becoming aware of the full-bodied love inside me. As he spoke to me through the screen in front of me, I could feel what he said was true.*

*"Ah, you like yourself!" I felt my face flush. My body was growing warm. Every nerve in my body was alive with electricity, my heart beating, blood pumping. I could hear myself breathing, the cells coming alive in my body. The warm tears fell soft against my cheeks – tears of joy.*

*"Yes, I do. I genuinely like myself. I AM a good person," I said as I wiped the tears from my face, smiling slowly, though not at him. The smile was at the beauty I saw in me – the woman on the screen before me.*

*Up to this moment in my life, it was my firm belief that loving myself was impossible. I did not like me, yet others would say, "I love you" to me. Couldn't they see the defects in character, the scars, the pain in my face?*

# One

## Learning to Lie

*"Is it still lying if something isn't said?"*
*~ Sher Unbound*

He was sitting next to me on the edge of the sidewalk, an alert that something was wrong. For the first time, I was fully and frighteningly aware of how much larger than me he really was. My awareness of his size compared to mine left me feeling small and powerless, as though he were some giant in his fresh uniform. I never felt this way while roller skating or playing in the yard with my cat. I could feel myself shrinking into something small and afraid the more he spoke.

Had he ever sat with me before this moment? This question raised my awareness of feeling smaller, nervous, and in a bit of panic as my small hands reached down, poking my fingers into the shoelaces. Picking at the little white laces in my shoes was a welcome distraction from the growing stomach pain I had become accustomed to in his presence.

My eyes stole a glance. Looking up, I noticed he wasn't looking at me. Instead, he was looking around him, turning his head side to side as though he were watching for someone. He reminded me of my cat when it watched the birds as they landed in the yard.

His tone of voice was serious, the kind of serious that told me something was wrong, or I was in trouble again. Still pulling at my shoelaces, looped around my index finger at this point, my thoughts were only on trying to keep my stomach from hurting, rocking a little back and forth – it was really beginning to cramp. What did I do? Was I in trouble? I was afraid to look at his face for fear it might match the tone in his voice.

My shoelaces becoming less of a distraction, I noticed the heat rising and stinging the backs of my bare legs. Feeling grateful for the distraction of shifting enough to move a tad away from his presence, my awareness turned away from everything. Away from the uncomfortable proximity of his much larger frame and my stomachache.

His voice was grave when he spoke. The tone, I know that tone. It's him about to spank me. My stomach was nagging at me that whatever this was, it must have been something bad – we never sit here. Only half-listening to him, I remembered what the spankings felt like by the strap he used. It was a belt that felt like it covered my entire buttocks with each slap. It made me clench and dance on my toes, trying to get away from his strikes. Each time I'd pee, and as it ran down my legs, he'd get angry at me, telling me it hurt him worse than it hurt me. How could it? How could anything hurt worse than being stripped and strapped with a belt until I couldn't stand it anymore? As I write this, I feel my butt cheeks clenching with the memory of what that felt like and dancing around in the effort to escape.

Was it his voice or what he was saying to me that made me feel so nervous? Was it that he was sitting too close to me here, where we never sit? Wait. He's asking me something. Pay attention, Sherri. He's asking me not to tell Mother about our playtime or this talk. Why can't I tell her? This isn't our secret playtime, and what is wrong about that time and this talk? Him telling me I could not tell Mother added to my confusion and nervous state even more. Who am I not supposed to tell what to, Daddy?

What he was saying to me was that I had to speak to a man about Mommy and tell the truth about what I saw, but not tell about our playtime. Why was he asking me all this? Why would I lie about what I saw? Why does this feel so uncomfortable? Why am I nervous?

As children, we seem to know instinctively about lying – unless you live a lie. Lying isn't lying if it's your reality, right? I held secrets and told lies as a child. But were they lies if you were told not to tell or talk about them? Maybe it was never discussed except between you and another child or adult. Maybe they were secrets like mine. The kind of secrets that made my stomach hurt; the kind of hurt that makes a person fold over with cramps. The kind of secrets that kept me locked up inside and ill for almost 60 years.

### *How did you learn about lying?*

*"There's great wonder when a child becomes aware*
*of their relationship to the world around them.*
*The saddest is when they learn to deny it."*
*~ Sher Unbound*

Dad, you taught me to never tell anyone about our secrets. It's a special secret. Never talk about what we do. My inner child begins to stir and her small voice that I no longer recognize speaks with understanding; my own voice drops in between her words. At times it's hard to tell the difference between her thoughts and mine.

"I understand, Daddy. I'll get in a lot of trouble if I tell. We don't tell anyone about our special playtime; the gist of what I repeated to you, so you knew I understood how to lie – or not lie. That confuses me because I don't lie. I get spankings for lying, right?"

You had me repeat everything to you, so you knew I understood. I knew not to question you. Nodding my head in cautious agreement, still fidgeting with my shoelaces, my stomach was beginning to hurt a lot. I let you continue without saying a word. Always listen to the adults and never disobey was another lesson you taught me. In the next few moments of my confusion, I realized you were asking me to lie by not telling anyone what you were doing to me.

You were saying it's okay to tell a lie on your behalf always but tell the truth about all else. You were saying, "If you love me, you won't tell the truth." Sadly, I did love you, and that love left me feeling twisted inside for nearly my entire life. How can I live a lie and tell the truth? I don't know how I did, but rest well – you were a good teacher.

I still don't understand getting the bare-butt spanking from you that I did for telling a lie another time. *You lied and nothing happened.* I lied and was spanked by you and then ignored until you wanted more pleasure.

Do you remember also telling me to never, *ever,* tell the people in the cold white courtroom about us? The room that echoed and made voices louder when people talked. The room with the floors that made the sound of people walking sound like they were stomping. The room that made me afraid of the sound of my own voice. The voice that was beginning to crackle with choked back tears as I spoke. I was too little to be doing your dirty work, Daddy.

When the judge asked me about my mother's boyfriend and to give exact moment-by-moment details of all that I did and saw, he first asked me if I knew what a lie was. I couldn't tell him, "No sir, that part confuses me," because then I would have had to tell him about our conversation on the sidewalk.

I looked at him and I turned to you, feeling confused, afraid, and anxious. My throat hurt from the tears I was holding in. My words were caught in my stomach, causing gut-wrenching pains. My bladder was telling me I needed to pee, but I couldn't leave the room.

Did you read in my eyes what I was asking? "Daddy, what do I say?"

I was groomed to lie against all instincts, goodness, and morals. I lied because I was told not to tell. I lied because no one taught me there were choices. No one gave me permission to say "no," especially to an adult. Always be good and never disobey was what I was taught. A good lesson with poor outcomes later in my life.

It never occurred to me to deliberately disobey, which would mean standing up for myself. Oh, the irony. Daddy told me that if I told our secret, Mother would leave me, and he would be sent away. And that is exactly what happened. I never told anyone that secret until I was much older. I only told the truth about my mother in the courtroom. I didn't have to lie about him because no one ever questioned his character.

I felt like a bad kid because in my mind I had done something awful. I told the man in court I was sorry I saw my mother and her boyfriend and that it was scary to see. He asked me if I understood what I saw under the covers. "No," I lied. She was doing the same thing Daddy did to me; you get naked together where no one sees you. Why did I feel so bad that I told the truth but not the whole truth of what I understood? Is the truth bad? My stomach hurt and I had to pee. Please, let me out of here. I want to go home now.

*At what point did you become aware of lying as a child or by omission?*

*"If you love me, you won't tell the truth."*
*~ Sher Unbound*

A montage of memories plays repeatedly in my head, almost like a movie. This movie is one I wish I could delete from the playlist forever.

The phone rang, startling me awake. My nervous system jumped into gear, reminding me of all my mother's rules. Answer the phone by the third ring, never wake her up on the weekends, only use half a cup of milk in our cereal, change the baby's diaper and feed her, let the cat out, do not go outside until after she wakes up and never, ever, EVER open her bedroom door.

"Hello," I answered, curious who was calling so early in the day.

"Is Roy there?" said the caller. "He's late for work."

Quietly, I looked around the room and into the living room, visible from where I was standing. I replied with some confusion, "Roy's not here."

Eyeing the living room for signs of his presence, I noted my mother's bedroom door was still closed but her silky oriental robe was tossed casually on the couch, raising an alert in my mind. The coffee table played host to partially filled wine glasses, an empty wine bottle, and a full ashtray. Her leather cigarette case and lighter were on the table, almost obscured by the array of clutter.

"Go wake him up. Have him come to the phone," he said, startling me back to attention.

"Okay, I'll check."

Setting the receiver on the counter, I went to the forbidden door and paused. The stomachache was coming back. I had a strong hesitant feeling standing outside her door. I knew to do what the caller instructed, but I also knew what would happen if I upset my mother.

Almost tiptoeing, I walked silently across the living room to her bedroom door, cautiously placing my ear next to the thin wood to listen. Holding my breath, terrified the heartbeat in my ears could be heard, I exhaled a moment and silently drew another breath. No sound came through the door. Exhale silently. Do I do this? Dare I open the door? What if she yells at me? What if I get spanked for snooping? I felt nauseated.

Drawing in and holding my breath again as though it would make the turn of the knob quieter, I placed my hand on the knob and turned. Click. My stomach jumped. Taking another deep breath, I turned the knob as slowly as possible with a near-death grip. In a slow-motion movement, the door opened.

Darkness draped the room. I wished I could see – I was afraid of the dark. The only thing visible directly before me was a form under the pile of blankets, but I couldn't see her. I needed a light.

I decided to walk backward out of her room leaving the door open. I was already being bold, why not leave the door blatantly open? Once I passed the doorway, my movements were quick and determined on my mission to retrieve the flashlight from the kitchen. Returning to her room with the light, my steps were near a sprint on my toes.

My breathing was slow and deliberate with every step. My stomach was hurting again – no, not now! I knew this was my chance to confirm my feelings that she was more interested in "him" than she was me. At that moment, I had nothing more than will to see what was in the dark.

Creeping quietly into her room, I swore she would hear me breathing, so I held it in. Filling myself with courage and determination, I crouched at the foot of the bed and turned on the flashlight. I drew in another deep breath and froze. Do I want to know? Yes! What was she doing and who was she with? With a count of three, I raised the covers and directed the light under them.

My eyes froze, then seemed to dart back and forth on their own, taking in the entire scene in front of me. She was sleeping in the nude and next to her was the bare body of a man, a man who was not my father. My thoughts raced with hurt, rejection, shock, and curiosity. My fear was verified. She loved "him" more than me and she didn't love Dad.

I dropped the covers of the bed, simultaneously deciding to drop the flashlight on purpose at the foot of her bed. I knew this would wake her up, and it did. She startled and sprung upright with a look of confusion on her face like the bride in horror films would. Mother focused on the noise, then must have realized it was me standing in her room, her nudity in full view. Mother squinted her eyes and began to protest, yelling at me, demanding to know what I was doing in her room while pulling the bedsheets over her bare body. Roy sat up next, looking bewildered, asking my mother what the problem was.

"She's standing right there, that's the problem. She saw us!" She exclaimed at the top of her voice. Holding the blankets to her chest in one hand, she waved a perfectly manicured hand in my direction. Standing there motionless, I was terrified to even blink, so I fixed my eyes into a glare back at her. I began to feel a little spiteful and simultaneously pleased with myself for creating chaos in less than the blink of an eye.

"Someone's on the phone for him," I said with defiance while I turned on my heel and walked out of the room with confidence. I knew exactly what I was going to do next. Mother yelled after me, "Get out and shut the damn door!" I didn't close the door and continued to walk to the phone receiver. The caller probably heard most of the commotion with such a small space we were living in. As I reached the receiver, I casually picked it up and hung it back on the base, disconnecting the call.

*What did you find out as a child you wish you never knew?*

*"The power of a mother can lift or crush."*
*~Sher Unbound*

The court hearing was finished, and a few minutes after, I packed my little overnight case. As fate would have it, my siblings and I were flying to California to stay with my grandparents. I took this as another one of the moves we made frequently with Dad's job. This time was different. There was a feeling of uncertainty about everything that had occurred. The courtroom, the men who spoke to me, my Dad's endless questions, the silence in the house. Nothing felt normal.

I was chatty when I was nervous (a behavior that never stopped). She was not packing; the house was still the same with all our things everywhere – like the cookie jar that held the Oreos where I learned the difference between "a couple" and "a few." That was one of the rare moments I recall her speaking to me. My mother saying almost nothing to me was normal, yet everything changed in a moment because of one fact. I told the truth. Was that bad?

The day we left is burned into my mind like a scene in a movie that plays repeatedly. I have lived my life trying to sort out if there was something I missed. Trying to ease my guilty conscience through the years, I created fantasies about what she might have felt on the day we left instead of facing the truth.

Truth. What is the truth? I have tried to remember her speaking to me about anything other than doing my chores, telling me to stop talking, or making fun of me for wetting my pants and bed. I told the truth, like she and Dad always told me to. I believed the stories I told myself; that her rejection punished me for life because I told the truth. The memories linger long after her death (about which I am still uncertain how I feel).

The loving stories of her that I created to soothe my wounds were all about reunions in magical places in faraway lands. Kings and Queens, parents rescuing children, handsome young princes dancing with maidens. Stories set in space, on distant undiscovered planets, fantasizing she would come find me, hugging me for the first time ever while we cried. (I never saw her cry or laugh – I just realized that.)

In my stories, she would look at me and tell me how sorry she was and how much she loved me. She would talk to me, smile at me, and be *my mom*. In every story, she was always forgiven with love and the understanding that she had simply made a mistake.

***What fantasy did you create to soothe yourself as a child? As an adult?***

*"For today, let us be kings and queens,*
*heroes and heroines."*
~ *Sher Unbound*

# Two

## Letters

*"The relationships end, but never my love."*
*~ Sher Unbound*

Sherri,

While working on the edits in this journal, it came to me there was one important person I forgot to mention. What was missing was my letter to you, my darling inner child.

The whole purpose of this book is to heal from the insane lifestyle you lived, but not as a child; you were treated as though you were born directly into adulthood. What started as an effort to reclaim personal power turned into a healing tool for others. You helped me find meaning in my life. Thank you, Sherri.

I've done the work that was needed for us to reintegrate with you, little one, and allow you the peace you deserve. It's time for your pain to end and for you to rest.

Half my life has been spent reading bestselling self-help books, viewing hours of videos, sitting through thousands of hours in therapy, lost in months of inpatient treatment, thousands of pills for psychological and medical diagnoses, consuming more alcohol than was necessary, and suffering through surgeries because of the abuse I put our body through – all to keep you safe. Was that really helping you feel safe? No. It wasn't, and I'm sorry for not taking care of you, my little one.

I'm sorry that as your adult self, it was me that kept you quiet because I bought into the lies told to me – the lie that how you were treated didn't matter. There were always rules to follow about what to lie about, what to say and not say. I'm coming into the awareness that those rules set you to grow with anxiety and self-doubt, never trusting the truth. Not once did I let you speak your feelings, your thoughts. I controlled those; just as you were controlled by our parents when you were so little.

Little one, it's hard to remember exactly when all the abuse began. There are only bits and pieces and it takes a lot of effort to put all the images together on a timeline. Some memories are quite vivid; like they happened yesterday. The more you stir in me, the more that returns to my memory. It's important for me to remember as much as possible so you feel secure and safe, and to know you never will be placed in any of those situations again.

There are good things I remember about you when you were alone or spent time with your grandparents. Music was a magical journey into a place other than where you were. When you asked if you could learn to play the violin because you loved the sound, you were told no, that you weren't smart enough to, so you gave up. As an adult now, the desire to play the violin or learn to play the mandolin is as strong as ever.

You did have a little fun as a child. Riding on the back of your brother's bike, hanging on with all your strength so you wouldn't fall off the seat. A favorite show was "The Mickey Mouse Club," and you enjoyed Warner Brothers cartoons that your babysitter let you and brother watch. Cartoons were not allowed in the parents' home, so it was a special treat to watch these.

I remember a few of your favorite toys – the iron horse with the broken tail that you held too tight until you wore the color off, exposing the green nature of the metal; the record player with all your favorite songs from the movies you never got to see, but you knew the songs by heart. Those songs are still in my heart, Sherri. I sang some of them to my children when they were little, and now our grandson watches the movies and musicals you were denied seeing as a child.

Something else you loved: the pretty glass-like Cinderella slippers that Nonnie gave you. They were plastic, but they clicked and sparkled like glass when you walked across the floor just like the grown-up ladies' shoes did. The way your little toes showed through the ends of the shoe was just like Cinderella's slippers. *That's where that name came from!* You always called them your Cinderella slippers.

You didn't have an easy time making friends. Shy of other kids after you were made fun of when your mom put you in diapers to go to school, you'd walk slowly so no one would notice the bulk under your snow pants, but it still showed. My heart breaks for you little one, and I'm sorry you were humiliated in that way.

Your new sisters were fun to be around, although like the other kids you wanted to play with, you didn't seem to quite fit in with them. Everyone told you to stop being so serious and be a kid. Funny, I say that to my grandson now. Inner pain has a strange way of taming the wild in us.

Do you remember how much you loved to sing? The fantasy you had of being a singer on stage one day, far away from anyone and no one could tell you stop making noise? Your favorite song to sing was "La la lu" from "Lady and the Tramp." Peggy Lee's voice is so soothing, even in this moment. Whenever I listen to those songs, tears pool in my eyes and my throat holds back any words from forming. I'm sorry you weren't rocked or held like you wanted to be. I'm sorry you were so alone, little one. You rocked yourself to sleep, played alone; brother played with you outside when he was in the mood.

You did the best you could for your mother. Sherri, you were so little and you tried to follow all her rules and never make a fuss around her. The massive amount of rules she demanded to be observed was overwhelming. You only wanted to please her so she wouldn't be so mad at you all the time. I'm especially sorry you had to hear those words she said to you, the names she called you. I believe she loved you but wasn't sure how to show it. She was hurt too, but couldn't express it.

We'll never know why, but she had to have loved you to be so hurtful with her words. It was only her protecting her heart, just as I've said words that hurt others to protect mine.

And then you learned how to lie from the adults responsible for you. You were in the very adult world of lies. These weren't the small lies kids tell, like if they break something and are afraid to tell the truth. These were lies that not even adults ought to know. They had no business putting you in the position you were in. I'm sorry you had to move through their world as rapidly as you did, growing from infant to adult at less than three years old.

You are safe. I hear everything you have to say. I see all the memories, so you don't need to see them anymore.

I'm learning to play, to have the fun we were meant to have as a child. I'm learning to feel again and allowing all those cold hard feelings you held within to come out and pass on. I've got this now, little one. It's your turn to smile, laugh, sing, and dance freely.

I love you, Sherri.

**What would you say to your inner child right now?**

*"I'm sorry, Please forgive me, Thank you, I love you."*
*Ho Oponopono Prayer*

Mom,

The stories played in my mind for most of my life about the day we left. Maybe you were too heartbroken to look at me. Were you embarrassed because you made a mistake? It's okay, Mom. I know about making mistakes. It never occurred to me to tell you that you should be ashamed of yourself like you always told me to be. I listened to you, Mom, and became ashamed of myself like you said.

You made a mistake, Mom, and I knew you did. I wasn't angry at you, and I was never ashamed of you. I didn't tell anyone about you and that man because of anger. I told my babysitter and asked her to help me understand because I was feeling confused about why you loved that man more than you loved me.

I never told you about what Dad was doing to me because he told me not to and you never seemed to mind what he was doing. You didn't seem to be upset when you curled my hair, put makeup on me, and dressed me like a grown-up lady so you and Dad could introduce me to strange men. Wasn't that telling the truth, or was that a lie? This whole "what is a lie" and "what is the truth" concept is terribly confusing to me.

Maybe that day we left you were angry at me for leaving you and broke the dishes you were washing on purpose when I said goodbye. Did you think I abandoned you, or that I rejected you for leaving with Dad? Anger wasn't ever a part of it, Mom; only my perception of feeling rejected carried for the rest of my life. I tried to get your attention and tell you I wanted to stay with you, but maybe the protests were not loud or clear enough.

My mind often trails off to a moment of fantasy, imagining that after we left you fell to the floor in dramatic waves of sobs, chest heaving while you tried to scream. Maybe you know that feeling?

The scream that is stuck inside and won't come out, like the one Munch painted, "The Scream." Even writing this to you, my imagination leads me to a scene of me curled into a ball on the floor, rocking and crying, releasing this pain.

Maybe you fell into the arms of your lover and cried on his shoulder for how you treated me. I understand that image now as a grown woman, except there is no lover whose safe chest and arms I can fall into. I have my thoughts and a pillow to cry into.

I told the truth and lost both you and Dad.

But then, perhaps you really meant every word you said. Maybe I needed to be ashamed of myself. Maybe I wasn't good enough to be your daughter. You were thin, a real beauty queen. Thin, petite but with big mean words. I was chubby, uncertain, and wet my pants, afraid and... maybe... I didn't deserve you as my mother.

After all, I ate one Oreo too many and didn't like pink ice cream. You became angry at me for telling you I didn't want to go with the man to Sunday School anymore, then more upset when I asked you why you weren't coming with me. Odd there is no memory of ever arriving at Sunday School. My words were not well received when my feelings about that man or him buying me pink peppermint ice cream were shared with you. My mere existence seemed to bring you anger.

You were standing at the kitchen sink in the small trailer home. Like always, you had your back turned to me and your hands were moving mechanically. Pick up the dish, wipe it, one side then the other, put it in the sink of clear water, then the next dish. Every now and then you would look up at the window in front of you above the sink. You would not turn around to look at me speaking to you. Wash, rinse, repeat.

Do you know that there is no memory in my mind of you smiling or crying? My strongest memory of you is from behind you. Was I ugly, Mom? Were you ashamed of me? Was I annoying when I spoke to you? Did I ask too many questions or have an ugly voice?

I took care of baby sis and tried to wash my sheets like you told me to; I cleaned her diapers in the toilet water, just like you said. I even found your jade earring that baby sister swallowed once and dug it out of her diaper before I rinsed it, just like you told me to.

My heart aches; I have so few memories left of you. What color were your eyes? I can close my eyes and see your hair, the profile of you driving and smoking Pall Mall cigarettes in your red Mustang, but I don't remember what color your eyes were. What color of lipstick was it that you wore all the time? Did you wear a fragrance? Most people know what fragrance their mother wore, and it brings back warm memories.

A fond memory of you was watching you fix your hair into the fancy French twist you wore. Your long and straight auburn tresses – you would wrap and pin them and use what seemed like enough hairspray to fill the bathroom. Watching you move around the house while you cooked or cleaned is one of the memories I recall with fondness, until the one comes up where you told me that I could do a better job at whatever it was that you were correcting me for. I wanted to be like you when I grew up. I loved you, Mother. More than you ever knew.

What's missing are the memories of you interacting with Dad, friends, or neighbors. They aren't there, but that doesn't matter – I only wanted you to look at me. I did a lot of silly things to get you to see me. Sing, create dances and jokes, but you never laughed with me. You didn't play with me; we barely spoke. I only wanted you to pay a little attention to me, other than spanking me or telling me to clean something up.

Sitting at the kitchen table by another window, my chatter was directed to you while I was fidgeting with something on the table. My hands were always busy because I always felt nervous in your presence. Wanting nothing more than to have you look at me was a feeling that I could never let go of.

As always, you were standing with your back to me and kept washing dishes as though your daughter was invisible. Your anger filled the room with so much heaviness. Feeling that there was something awful I had done was exacerbated by your silence. Were you going to spank me again? Would you tell me what a bad girl I was and how ashamed of myself I needed to be? Why wouldn't you talk to me?

Dad broke my one-sided idle chatter with myself by saying it was time to go. Rising slowly from the table, I remembered to push my chair in. It was proper to always push our chairs in when we left the table. Walk quietly, don't "plod." Cows plod, ladies glide – I remembered to walk like you told me to, Mom. In my best effort, with all of the determination and courage in me, I did something I never did before; I breached the barrier you told me never to cross because I desperately needed you to hug me. I needed you to tell me you were sorry, and I wanted to tell you I was sorry for telling the truth. I needed my mom to love me.

My words were in my throat, holding back the tears welling up inside me, ready to burst out. When my hand reached up to tap your arm, you flinched as if you were burned by my touch. That startled me and made me stand in my place. I didn't touch you again. "Mommy, I love you. Can I have a hug?" It felt like an eternity before you spoke. You continued washing the dishes – wash, rinse, repeat, never looking at me. I held my arms up in vain for what felt like an eternity, just wishing with all my being you would hug me, look at me, LOVE me. You spoke into the dirty dishwater, and to the dishes you said, "I hate you. I never want to see you again."

I wonder, were you speaking to the dishes or to Dad? You didn't mean that Mommy, right?

**What do you need to let go of?**

*"Sherri Matters."*

Dearest Sister,

The airplane ride was filled with tears and confusion. Noisy, stale, and cramped. I held you on my lap the entire flight. The hot, smoke-filled air choked me as much as my tears were choking me.

Throat dry, I was offered a can of 7-UP, which seemed to help a little. My seat was next to Dad, who I wished wasn't there. He told me several times to stop crying and making noise and to keep you, little sister, quiet. Why was Dad so angry at me? I told the truth. His irritation was creating so much confusion in me.

Our brother wasn't saying a word. He only looked out the window of the jet, like a stone. Feelings of shame and rejection washed over me repeatedly, for being who I was; a naughty little girl who hurt people. Sad and confusing thoughts pushed through the noise of the plane and passengers. I wondered if this was what my life was to be: ignored and silenced. Those feelings didn't leave until just before writing this journal. It was my belief all these years that my purpose was only to serve as a whipping post and doormat for others, never to be recognized for being honest, good, and obedient.

My excitement was subdued when I saw our grandparents, which was sad because normally there would be joy. I loved our grandparents dearly, but it was our parents my heart wanted. Wishes never come true. I gave up wishing this all would go away with a blink of the eyes like a magic trick. Wishes for never having been born, of course, never came true.

My body had no more tears and left me dry enough to make my head hurt. Every noise was muffled from my ears ringing. Why did it feel like it was my fault this mess was happening? I didn't do anything except answer the phone and tell my babysitter. I told the man in the court the truth as I had been instructed, and now Dad seemed so mad at me. More wishes passed through my mind, wishes I had never been born.

Our grandmother was animated with joy and showed us children to the room that we would call "our room" for the next two years. The room smelled old. Brother's bed was on one side of the room, mine opposite his and your baby crib in between by a window covered over with plastic.

The house wasn't the pretty house Mom made for us. Everything was covered in thick plastic. We were shown all the things in the house to never touch. More rules. More fake. Nothing was real anymore. I felt myself fade away. I recall hoping I could shrivel up like the dead moth lying at the base of the window that was trapped by the sheet of plastic.

No doll, no records, my bed and my friends were not there, and I was wondering what happened to my cat. Who would feed him and play with him? That first night, I cried myself to sleep after what was received as admonishment by our grandfather for asking to have a light on. "Big girls don't need the lights on to sleep," he said.

Our brother spoke to me for the first time that day. "Quit being such a baby. If you had kept your mouth shut, Mom would still be with us."

Have you ever cried so much that you were dry? Only a deep, dry ache in your bones? Something happened to me that day. It wasn't only moving away; it was a removal of my spirit. How far away can a soul be buried before life is snuffed out? That's how far I made mine go.

I'm sorry I left you behind the day I ran away. That moment has played in my mind so many times over the years. You were standing there in your room playing, asking where I was going. There are moments the word "abandoned" crosses my mind when the memory comes. I know you were afraid of being left alone and uncertain of what I was saying to you.

There was no choice but to leave you because taking you with me could have made a giant mess of both our lives. My heart wanted to grab you and run far away and take care of you as I always had, until our new family arrived. Leaving you was the hardest thing I ever had to do, but it was the best choice. You know

now why it was necessary to leave and have found the truth for yourself as well.

You've had a lot to face alone in that house all those years. I have some awareness of what you were challenged with through the little we shared when you and I reconnected. I can't imagine what you felt like when you were told our new mom was not who gave birth to you. I'm trying to fit together the pieces of our life before our new family, so I can assist you in putting some of your life back together.

You were an easy baby to take care of until you began having seizures. I never knew why you started them, only that they were scary to me. Knowing how to help you with them was out of my realm of experience and I could only watch you suffer through them while you thrashed in my arms. You were quiet mostly, so it made no sense to me that you were so unhappy as a toddler after we moved in with the new family. *What happened?*

Watching you grow into a beautiful, spiritual woman has offered me so much joy. You launched your successful career while raising your three beautiful babies. It makes my heart proud to know their values are as deep and strong as yours. My love for you grew as you stood your ground, unlearned the messages taught to you, and held to your convictions. You are an inspiration to me, dear sister.

There are decisions we make that are by choice, yes, but sometimes they are planned by destiny. My choices haven't all been the best, but one choice that was made for which I am forever grateful is that I left you there in the room that day, with a promise to return for you.

That day came, and while we are separated by the miles, I am here for you always. For now, let us love and cherish one another, hold each other up, and be the women we were meant to be. Proud Spirit Warriors, leaving no one behind on their journey.

**What do you need to tell your siblings, your family, or your inner child?**

*"Just love Me."*
*~ Sher Unbound*

Brother,

What was your pain like? Is that why you are estranged? Have you done what so many of us do and shut the world out, or have you opened and created a new life? My wishes and hopes are that you are safe, well, and loving toward yourself.

If time could be turned back, would it have made our lives different? Worse? We can only imagine what would have been. We can't turn it back; all we have is now.

Brother, my new school was frightening and large and left me feeling alone. It was confusing to find my way when you normally would have been there with me to show me what to do. There were so many more kids in this new school that getting lost in the crowd was easy. I needed you, brother, and missed having you help me figure out my next steps. Please be patient with me as you walk with me through a short version of what life was like for me without my older brother.

Concentration was not my best trait, which proved to be embarrassing as well as other moments. Questions went through my mind all day, lasting into the night. I fidgeted quite a bit, always being told to sit still, stop shaking my legs, put my hands down, don't jiggle so much; maybe you remember all of this.

This question needs to be asked. What made you and Mom so angry with me? I told the truth and you both seemed angry with me. Was I supposed to lie in court, or keep quiet? Maybe you are right that if I had told a lie to the man in the room that day, maybe we would have Dad and Mom and our family. Maybe we would be back home safe with our babysitter and friends. Did you miss our babysitter too? It's odd how I can remember more about their family than I can about our own mother.

Did you know how alone, lost, and unloved I felt? I missed you then and I miss you now. We tried to connect over the years, but after Dad passed you went silent. What made you go so invisible, dear brother?

The kids in the new school were harsh. They made fun of me for my clothes, for my developing breasts, for being such a quiet and serious kid, and for being the "new kid." It didn't help my reputation much the day I peed in class.

It wasn't my fault, brother. The teacher would not call on me when I raised my hand to use the restroom. Holding my arm up while trying to hold my bladder, the thought of walking out of the classroom crossed my mind. Finally, I made the decision not to do it, because the last time I did she slapped the tops of my hands hard with a book.

I crossed my legs and wiggled in my seat back and forth, side to side, and when it couldn't be held much longer, I blurted out that I needed to use the restroom. She scolded me, saying I was being rude and selfish by interrupting her. It was right then my bladder let go, spilling pee on the floor below my seat. My bladder was relieved, but my red face and immediate tears marked me for the rest of the school year as "Peepants." The walk to the principal's office was a long and shameful one.

Dad told me what would happen if I lied or told the truth. That was too confusing for me, and it still is; this was my punishment for what again? No one told me my childhood was over. Dad went on deployment for what seemed an eternity and there was no contact with Mother. No friends, just you, my only brother, and our baby sister.

Dearest brother, you barely spoke to me. I missed you so much and you were right there in the room with me. Our baby sister was always crying like me, except I learned to cry inside, no longer allowing my tears out. That lesson was taught well in school. Crying only draws attention. Learning to become invisible was easy. I believed if I was forgotten I may as well make myself unseen and insignificant, much like the dead moth trapped behind plastic.

If only I knew which lie to tell and to whom, this would never have happened. Maybe the truth is we all lie, and I had not learned that yet.

*What do you blame yourself for in your life? It wasn't your fault.*

*"Maybe the truth is we all lie."*
*~Sher Unbound*

Pop,

I wish… I wish I would have told you when you were on earth exactly what a hero was to me. You were and are my definition of a hero. Rough around the edges with the heart of a Spirit Warrior, like me. You taught me well, Pop, about life. You were the only one who showed me unconditional love before I knew what that meant.

The knowledge you weren't my blood grandfather wasn't shared with me until years later, but through my eyes, it didn't matter. You loved me. You always showed me respect. You spoke to me, and you hugged me without condition or expectations in return. No other adult did.

The afternoon coffee shop visits for cocoa and coffee and a glazed donut, long chats about school life, imparting your wisdom to me about how to get along there and keep some dignity. Those coffee shop chats helped me learn how to add faster, how to order from a restaurant, why we tip waitresses, and the importance of manners.

The stories you shared about being a Marine, what you did in the war, and how the city has changed kept me on the hook, wanting to know more of your amazing world. I learned to appreciate our men in uniform because of you and the pride you held in serving our country. You showed me what having pride is when you introduced me every time in the coffee shop, saying, "This is my granddaughter," and smiled while you placed your big hand on my shoulder.

Everything you did for me was a lesson in something. The chats while helping you in the vegetable garden, teaching me values in life through growing tomatoes and fruit trees. The long rides around town showing me how to find my way home if I got lost. Listening to me tell you about my troubles with math and you helping me by counting rubber bands, paper clips, and other magical items you would always "just happen to have handy" in your pockets.

You smiled great big smiles every time I would put on a dance show like the dancers on Lawrence Welk, and we'd laugh every time he said, "and a one, and a two, and a tree…" – then we'd pop our mouths and make the champagne bottle sound. These are precious memories to me. Were you aware of the influence you had over me in areas of academics, the arts, our country, and appreciation for what we have in our lives?

You weren't religious and I appreciated you for that. You didn't like that I was having to go to a Catholic school, and your dislike felt like sweet validation each time you told Nonnie, "Let her be a kid, Chic. She will be grown up too soon." I always knew you had my back no matter what, because of our loyalty to one another.

You told me to always be true to myself and how proud you were that I learned what truth is. Your strong belief in me was empowering, especially when you recognized and accepted me for being just me. You heard me tell you about my troubles in school, and never once told me to suck it up. You just listened and said to keep being true to myself. You were the first to accept me unconditionally. Awkward, skinny, shy Sherri.

Pop, you'd be so proud of your grandchildren and great-grandchildren. The same lessons you taught me and the times they spent in the garden with you gave them the same memory of the man you were – the hero to each of us.

You were the one to tell me, "I'm proud of you." You were proud when I made my break from the abuse. We all made it, Pop, and while I still struggle with healing, you are always in my heart and my head – whispering to me, "Keep going." I love you, Pop. My only wish is that I would have modeled my life more like yours. But then, would I be learning now what you taught me then, or would I know how to be my own hero?

I miss you, Pop.

**Who is a hero in your life?**

*"Heroes are unafraid
to be authentic and vulnerable."*
~*Sher Unbound*

Nonnie,

Your love for me was never a question. You and Pop tried to give us a home that we could rest in after the traumatic situation we kids came from. Your attention was special, and you helped me feel welcome.

The realization of how underappreciated and overwhelmed you probably felt while taking on three children at your age is coming to me now as I raise one of my own grandchildren. I never understood you until I began writing this journal and putting deep thought into how much love you shared with me in your unique way.

There is a sweet spot in my heart for the pet name you gave me, *"Garden of Roses."* To this day, that phrase remains in my heart. I know you meant well with all your efforts in trying to make me happy. You knew my heart was hurt and maybe we both were afraid but didn't know how to help each other. I never told you how to help because of my own uncertainty of what I needed. Just so you know, the pet name has helped me in my most anxious moments. Rose Water is my go-to scent when an extra dose of love is needed.

You must have felt embarrassed and taken by surprise by me when I shared with you my need for a bra because the kids at school were teasing me for having breasts. You scolded me for "having such unladylike language." The subject was not brought up again between us. In place of a bra, I wore several undershirts layered to prevent my budding breasts from showing.

You tried to teach me things you knew young women would face at my age before I decided to run away from home. When you would visit us as we kids grew older, you tried to tell me about pregnancy, to always be independent, and what careers would help me travel the world. Those conversations come to mind with thoughts of you. I have no regrets for my life, but it would have served me well to have listened more.

My mind filled with wonder when you shared your stories of your adventures working as a "Rosie Riveter," your days as an equestrienne, the places you and your sisters traveled for adventure as young women. You were trying to share with me what you knew I was capable of, except I was so hungry for love and affection for my mother that I ignored most of the lessons.

You tried to teach me how to be a lady and how to make a life for myself, independent of the rule of men. Proudly, these lessons are serving me well on my journey. You remained a strong influence in my life even after your passing. I feel the approval of myself and of you and Pop with your quiet, mannerly strength.

Nonnie, I am aware I broke your heart many times. I lashed out at people I loved most because I trusted you to understand my pain somehow. You didn't have it easy either growing up, and now the lessons you shared with me can be used to make a difference in my life. My life has not been a waste, not even my angrier youthful years.

Truth be told, you were quite the progressive for a woman of your time. I think of you daily and often wish we could sit together as women, chatting about the important things in life.

I'm listening now, Nonnie. I love you.

*What do you admire most about the women in your life, past and present?*

*"Doors don't always close to hurt.*
*They can close on Hope."*
*~ Sher Unbound*

My Dearest New Mom,

There comes a point in our lives when we feel the need to resolve our anger.

My anger was directed at everyone because I believed that both of my mother figures had rejected me. Releasing that anger took so much of my waking life, trying to reconcile in my mind what I meant to you both.

I wanted to be loved. As an adult, I know that now; as a child, I didn't know what it was.

You, my biological mother, my grandmother, my new auntie... all the women in the family held my admiration. It was my wish that someone would be as proud of me as they were of their own child, that I could stop short of becoming a nuisance in my eagerness to gain your attention.

Nothing seemed to catch anyone's attention; nothing seemed to please you, or at least that's how it felt, and in moments yet to this day. I wasn't funny, pretty, smart, or fast in school. I wasn't musically talented like my new sisters. The men thought I was good at sex; there was that for the attention I craved.

My love ran deep for you in my childhood and dearly as a grown woman. You are intelligent, classy, a sharp dresser, talented in your creativity. You sing, can play piano, and are an impeccable woman from all outward appearances.

You hold your own demons, and perhaps you have finally put some of them to rest. I don't know. You stopped communicating with me again, and once more I feel the painful question of, "What did I do this time?"

When I ran away from home, my sister told me how much it hurt you, but you had to know what was going on. How could you not? But then again, how could you? That's coming from me, a woman whose own children were being sexually abused by their biological father, just like I was. Not knowing all of this is understandable; perhaps you did know and blocked it out. Confusion on this point sets in when I think of the moment of the first red flag of sexual abuse happening to my children and took measures to keep them safe. Would you tell me if you did know all these years later, Mom? Would it make a difference?

I don't want to think that it was jealousy you felt toward me, but what other answer was there for not telling me you were proud of me for never giving up, for always trying even when the results were obvious I was not going to achieve the goals I set as a kid?

Instead, what I got from you was the silver tongue. A compliment followed with a "but…" Mom, could you just once tell me you are proud of the courage I have to survive and keep going? Proud of who I am as a woman? Proud that I am not leaving anyone behind, that I had the courage to step up into womanhood and stand on the truth and believe in myself?

I was apprehensive and excited when Dad met and married a woman with three children. *That woman was you.* In the blink of an eye, we were all moving into a home with a new family of two new sisters, a new brother, and a new mom. Along with this family came new grandparents, aunts, uncles, and cousins.

Life seemed like it might be a bit happier with my new family, if only I could feel less awkward and find something about me I liked. I never knew the right thing to say, and I didn't understand half the jokes, music, or activities this family did. I was unobservant and absorbed in comparing myself to my new siblings, picking out my faults to pay attention to the full meaning of what was to come. I missed my brother, who was present but with no care for my existence, and I was feeling more invisible as the years moved on.

Then there was the bladder control problem that was, as I now understand it, a result of being sexually abused. My temper was out of control to the point that in anger one afternoon, I stabbed my older sister with a fork in her arm, kicked in cabinets, and broke things on purpose. Angry, defiant, and unaccepting was my attitude. My lying was increasingly uncomfortable and never exceptionally good. I gave myself away when I lied because eventually it would eat at me until I spoke the truth, though I never shared the truth about my feelings. Feelings were meant to remain hidden and safe from others who wanted to use them. Feel nothing and there is nothing to lie about. Lying by omission, right?

On occasion, my biological mother would call to say she was coming to visit me. Elated for the day she came to visit, each time I would wait outside on the front steps of the house, watching anxiously to see who was in each car that passed. If there was a need for me to move or leave my post, it was my routine to ask one of my siblings to please let me know the second she arrived. She had the address because I heard you give it to her over the phone.

Sometimes a call from my bio mom would come, usually in the summer, and I would wait outside on the front steps of the house. The sun reached higher and hotter as it positioned itself in the sky, heating the cement of the front steps where I would sit. I didn't care. I didn't want to miss her driving into the driveway. She might think I wasn't home and leave.

No, I must sit here and wait... and wait... and wait.

"It's getting late, Sher. Let's call her and see if maybe something came up," you said.

"No. She said she's coming, I believe her."

It's inching toward evening now. "Did she call?" I'd ask as you joined me outside. Sometimes you sat with me in silence; other times you would talk to me about things I liked to do or chatter about the day.

"She's not coming, is she?" I'd ask you.

"No, I'm afraid not. Maybe something came up."

Those evenings, as the door closed behind me, the door to hope that maybe she was just busy, I finally believed what my bio mom had said. She hated me and never wanted to see me again.

Those moments were moments you gave me compassion and understanding, only moments.

I used to believe I had abandoned my little sister when I ran. My other sisters left soon after me, but my baby sister – my biological sister – I left her the night I had to leave. I thought she would be safe. Telling her she should have and play my records until I came for her helped me feel she'd be okay. Only I never came back for her.

My running away hurt you, Mom; Sis told me how you ripped my posters off the family photo wall. I had always imagined it was the same pain I felt when my bio mom told me she hated me, the feeling of abandonment.

It seemed I was always hurting you, even as an adult. No matter what my accomplishment was, there was always something that could be better or some improvement I could make. I never knew if you were proud of me for making it this far. Had I asked you if you were proud of me? Yes, I had and you responded with, "I love you, *but* you struggled with…"

Overall, you were good to me. You taught me to sew when other activities and skills seemed a lost cause, and we discovered there a knack for this time-honored skill. You were there for most of my firsts and helped me through some hard challenges in my life, but no matter how much I tried, I feel there was a time nothing I did would have met your expectations. *Maybe it was the expectations of myself I was not proud of.*

As the years passed, lying turned into something I did for survival, and you didn't understand any of it. My mindset when I did lie was one of the beliefs; it was normal for me. I had long since forgotten I was lying to myself about my feelings for survival.

I lied for Dad so I could protect you, Mom; I lied to you for *your* sake. There was never any intention to hurt you. I went so far as to lie to you about why I ran away at sixteen, telling you I was pregnant by a boy I had sex with (a huge lie!) and to prevent shame from being brought to you and Dad. Sis and I created that story. The ache to tell you stayed with me for years after running away. Only when I did, it was almost too late. Instead, the truth was buried and I hid my growing confusion and shame for another 21 years before I was brave enough to tell. *I only wanted you to love me.*

For me, it became easy to lie because I know what happens when we tell the truth – we lose. Mom, there is nothing more than my deepest love for you; however, I needed to write this journal knowing you won't be proud of my work here. Maybe you will understand the courage it took to write it and publish my story. I understand your views and your beliefs and respect them; however, this is for me. I know you loved me in your way, and I must accept that is enough.

**What made you believe you were responsible for your trauma?**

*"The truth is never for anyone's sake but your own."*
*~Sher Unbound*

# Three

## The Real Lolita

*"I should never have to work for love."*
*~ Sher Unbound*

How do children know to assign meaning such as pain or fear surrounding sexual abuse? Until we understand language at the approximate age of two, we have no concept of the meaning of actions or words other than what physically hurts. Of course, when a child is hurt, they cry. If they are yelled at, they cry because it startles them.

Touch is a different bird altogether. How do we understand what touch is without emotions being assigned? There is an entire existential conversation we could hold surrounding the question of perception and reality, but let's not.

When you are physically touched and words of love accompany that act, you learn to equate specific touches with specific words. When a child is touched while being spoken to, they learn to associate the meaning of those words with the touch and vice versa. Love = Sex. On the other hand, if you are told you are bad and stripped naked to be spanked, you are equating nakedness with "bad" and shame. Naked = Bad. Do you see where this is going? We assign meanings of words through actions as children. A child learns to associate acceptance or rejection through touch, tone, and words.

Through months of intense, daily inner work, among other skills, I learned to reassign meanings to the memories of my abuse. As a child, I absorbed the expectations and shame of my parents through their words and actions. It was a false belief I held for most of my life that what happened to me was deserved, having been born into the world as a "bad" person. Living with that belief made following their rules and requests easier because I thought if I could do enough good things to make them happy, I would turn into a good girl (sort of like Pinocchio).

Obviously, at one time or another, my tolerance for the physical pain created by the sexual manipulation of my body as a toddler increased. Oddly, there are only a few memories of anyone having been physically violent with me, other than the physical and sexual abuse by my father and others and some physical punishment by both my mothers *(except for the dream of the white house, which I may never know the answer to).*

*There is a recurring dream I have. The dream has reduced in recent months and is beginning to fade some recently. I'm little, not school age. I'm wearing a white dress. A man is with me, and all I can see are his greyish-brown slacks and shiny black shoes as we walk through the woods to a run-down white house.*

*Inside the house is crooked. The floors are broken tile and some wood shows. It feels tilted, as though it's off-balance, or I am. Then I am laying on the floor, face up. I can only see the walls with yellowed peeling paper, stained; it feels dirty. I have a difficult time seeing the man I am with.*

*Next, we are leaving the house. It's hard to walk because of the dizzy or tilted feeling. I only see the gravel we are walking on to return to a car that was not there at the beginning of the dream. It's a white car, long. My dream ends right there each time. I've never been able to explain it, or why I have had this dream most of my life. Key parts of the dream are: broken home, off-balance, a man, and a sense of not knowing where or who I am.*

There was no emotional meaning of sex due to my young age and lack of understanding. My body responded to physical touch in the way nature intended, but there was no awareness of it being "wrong." Being groomed to accept this behavior at an early age, I grew to believe for many years this was what was done between parents and their children. It was as normal for me as a hug would be to children not being sexually abused.

I was not aware until my early adolescence that something was deeply wrong with the sex and the lies that went with it. There was a vague inkling beginning to form that something was wrong, but I was unaware of the illegality of the sexual acts by my father and others. Confusion and questions in my mind were beginning to create a conflict, with mixed emotions of jealousy, how my body was responding, and experiencing the enjoyment of the way my body felt at times when it responded to touch. While it felt good, it felt wrong at the same time, leaving me feeling deeply conflicted. Was something wrong with me?

*If you don't know something is wrong until you are told it is, was it wrong before you knew?*

*"Enter understanding; Exit Blame."*
*~ Sher Unbound*

How do we learn to trust? We learn to trust what we know to be factual in our environment by the meaning we assign it. For me, sex as a child was normal and was to be trusted. As I began to explore my own awareness in my pre-teens, my understanding of what was true was beginning to disappear.

The messages I told myself were based on the belief I must have done something to entice his behavior toward me. The abuse I received caused me to develop shameful feelings toward myself. No one was telling me the way my body reacted was bad or good, nor did the reactions it produced ever feel bad; quite the contrary. They felt good, and the fact they felt good but no other girls were speaking of such things made me begin to doubt if I was normal.

No one told me I had the option to say no or tell another adult. I was simply not taught nor told there was a choice. Until my awareness developed a conflict of emotional pain and pleasure about the uncomfortable feeling in my body, it was normal to me.

There was constant conflict about not telling anyone. On one hand, tell the truth always, but on the other hand, never tell about the sex. Back to the question at hand, how do we learn to trust when we don't understand the complexity of lies versus truth? The truth of the matter is this: while it wasn't my fault my father sexually abused me, I assigned the meaning that I was bad early on (Naked = Bad). I trusted that meaning to be the truth, but nothing was farther from the truth.

What possible reason was there for doing this to me – the verbal and sexual abuse – unless I deserved it? The truth is he wasn't doing this "to" me. It was him projecting his own pain and shame on me.

But not knowing that as a child, my beliefs as I grew older were what I felt must be the truth.

I carried that belief for the next 45-plus years of my life. As I grew past my runaway years, the feeling of blaming myself for everything that happened to me and being ashamed of who I was grew with intensity. There was a time when my shame extended to being female. I saw myself as nothing more than a "bad seed," something that was abnormal or misplaced.

***What are you distrusting of? Where did that begin?***

*"We are not who we think we are."*
*~ Sher Unbound*

The sexual abuse was increasing in frequency, sometimes several times a day. Feelings of shame about my body were growing exponentially, along with shame around the physical response my body gave to the now-conditioned touch cues. How was I learning to understand all this? Not by emotional maturity, but through instinct. I knew something was abnormal about the behavior when it was paired with the embedded message of "don't tell."

I hated my body, how it felt, how older boys and men would stare. It was embarrassing to go swimming because of the comments made about the size of my breasts. This was alleviated sometimes by wearing a shirt over my swimsuit, so it was less obvious to me; however, a clingy wet t-shirt made my figure more obvious.

The frequency of the sexual stimulation was creating other side effects as well, such as an eating disorder, and my bladder control was worsening. Anorexia and bulimia, sleeplessness, poor concentration, irritability, anxiety, nail-biting, and bed-wetting were my life beyond school. I overdressed in larger clothing, as plain as I could.

I hated my natural physical reactions. At the time, there was so much uncertainty surrounding what was wrong with my body. The convulsions it made, the way my skin would get goosebumps and then shudder. I hated every moment of it, yet I enjoyed the pleasure of the very way my body reacted. There were times when I sought the pleasurable sensation by allowing other grown men to grope me, knowing there was pleasure to be found, and I would entice my father at times into making my body respond to the painful pleasure. I know that as a sexually abused child, I had limited, if any, boundaries.

There was an erotic taboo about leveraging my body to get what I wanted or needed from men. Sometimes, that was simply to have an orgasm for my enjoyment; other times it was to punish men. This was particularly effective in escaping punishment. The spankings stopped and grounding was almost unheard of. If I was in trouble, my father handled it without anything more than allowing him access to his prize. Sometimes his pleasure was punishment for me.

Later, I developed an awareness of how to arouse my father and other men sexually by walking, sitting, or bending a certain way, and I had the know-how to move when I sensed they were becoming aroused. "Tease" is the word that comes to mind; I learned how to use that skill to my advantage. There is genuine power in using sex, but it comes with a great price to a girl's self-worth. Before my mind could fully understand the meaning of everything, men were using me for what they sought: to have sex with a young, attractive, and highly seductive child. I thought this was *love*, since that word was usually uttered at some point.

**What do you offer yourself compassion and understanding for?**

*"Don't say you love me."*
*~ Sher Unbound*

It's odd how looking back on it, I am sorry my shape got away from me so much by gaining the excess weight. Of course, the abuse brought about shame for my body; I felt it had betrayed me, and the secret I believed was my obligation to carry.

I want to provide context to this truth. I developed a sensual and voluptuous figure a full year before I was biologically intended to, as my hormones reacted to the stress from sexual stimulation.

Betrayed by my body is what I felt. My body was betraying what my mind was trying to tell me was not a good thing. I was a bad girl; awfully bad for doing what felt good. Shame had taken its ugly fingers and wrapped them around my self-worth.

The first time I felt ashamed of my body was in the third grade as my breasts began to develop, leaving me uncomfortable and awkward. The whispers from the girls burned my ears and cheeks red with the shame of their audible whispers; I hated their questions about "what's sticking out of your shirt?"

Sixth grade: a teacher and a few boys were more than happy to comment on my ample breasts and hourglass figure. Not only was this awkward, but at that age, I recognized there was something men wanted from me.

After the teacher had his hands in my panties on a few occasions, the idea came to me if I were to wear jeans to school, his advances and interest could be stopped. Of course, that only turned attention toward my large breasts. My transformation from voluptuous to frumpy had begun before hitting what normal teen girls experience about body shame.

***What about your body or features are you afraid to love or embrace?***

*"The crime against girls is teaching them to be
ashamed of their bodies."*
~ Sher Unbound

It was easy to remain in my father's good graces by opening my legs in response to his touch when he wanted. For a considerable length of time, I had the mistaken belief that it was me who held the upper hand; however, ultimately, he proved to me I was not in control of anything.

Eventually, his desire for sex wasn't so covert. He had developed little signals. Touching my butt was a signal he wanted to play. If he brushed his swollen pants against my hand, he wanted his property. He had me trained like a dog – reach down to pet a dog and it rolls over and exposes its stomach to be scratched. I was aware of his signals and knew if I was in trouble or if there was something tangible for me to gain, I could use sex to get what I wanted.

The feeling was stirring in me about the age of 12 or 13 years old that something about all of this was not right. I was conflicted emotionally and physically. There was a growing awareness in me that it felt good to watch horny men squirm and shift uncomfortably if I sat too close to them or allowed them to play in my panties in public places, but there was also the feeling that something was very, very wrong with everything that was being allowed. I was aware there was something wrong with this behavior – theirs and my own.

*If any of this was right or normal, why was I always told to lie about it?* But I also knew that the only way to maintain my power and receive attention in any way possible was to allow my body to react in natural ways when touched sexually. Conversely, it was easy learning to withhold sex from my father when I needed leverage or felt unfairly punished. Innocent wickedness.

Sex is a powerful tool when used as leverage. That's not a behavior any child needs to know, even for survival. He stole my virginity, but he never stole my wild spirit or determination.

**When and for what have you used sex as leverage?**

*"Breaking a child's spirit is worse than death."*
*~Sher Unbound*

Thinking about my father as a man, a parent, a provider, a friend to others who did not know this side of him is a mind warp. It seems he was more than who he was when he was alone with me. At times I felt like a mistress, other times a stranger. When I heard about the number of people who attended his funeral, I was astonished!

As a provider, he worked hard to give us the comforts any American middle-class family could want. A well-kept home, nice things, good cars, a nice neighborhood – a classic "nice" middle-class family. As a father, when he was home, there are few memories of lessons, things he taught us as teens. Perhaps he spoke more with my brothers, but my memories are mostly filled with the growing burden of sexual abuse.

My awareness of morality was skewed, and feeling like a wicked child carried forward well into my adult years. It felt good to be aroused, to achieve waves of pleasure inside my body even as young as I was, while at the same time the memory of what I know now was abuse is burned into my memory and would replay every time I had sex in the years after. I had assigned the meaning to those memories that I was a bad person.

Physical development came early for me, but my emotional development was stunted. It came to me later to question the morality of all the situations while living in my parents' home. We don't need to think about "if" something is wrong – I believe we know instinctively.

There is one other memory that has bothered me ever since it happened. One night, while my date and I were parked in the driveway of my parents' house, we were talking, saying goodnight, and he leaned over to kiss me, so, like any other kiss, I began instinctively kissing him back. Out of the corner of my eye, flickering porch lights caught my attention – my signal to come in. Looking up, I saw my new mom standing at the door waiting for me to come in. It wasn't my curfew yet, but all right, I'd go in.

As I stepped inside the door, she grabbed me by the back of my hair, near my neck, and forced me down the stairs to my room. With her hand on my hair, she whipped me around, landing a hand across the side of my face. Shocked, I stood for a moment and without thinking slapped her back. That was a mistake that registered instantly with me the moment my hand landed, but it all happened so fast I couldn't have stopped if I wanted to. I don't know what possessed me to do that other than anger and confusion over her reaction. Was she acting this way because I kissed a boy?

We threw a few more punches and slaps at one another while she called me a whore several times, telling me how ashamed she was over my making such a display in public, kissing in the car like that; the neighbors would be horrified to see me acting this way. There it was. She was ashamed of me. I was a whore.

I've often wondered in the last few years if that was because she knew then what my father was doing to me. Was she aware and believed it was my fault? Was I really what she thought of me, a whore? Was she right?

That memory and others clouded my thinking for dozens of years after.

*You are not your past.*

*What beliefs are you allowing to control you?*

*"I am not my feelings."*
*~ Sher Unbound*

Though school was my favorite place to be in junior high, it was hard for me academically. I had to work harder to stay focused on my studies due to the growing confusion about the abuse paired with my normal hormonal growth.

At about the age of 15 or 16 years old, there was a way to not be around home much. After-school and summer activities became appealing excuses to escape. Anything that could be done after school to stay away from the house was fair game for me. In the summer, if I wasn't at the pool, beach, or doing chores, I was babysitting or at the mall.

I was always uncomfortable in my own skin and felt as though there was no real place I belonged. There were times I believed people could see inside of me and see how dirty my soul was. It made sense to me that the more I ignored my body and my feelings, the better off I was. It was a growing fight to keep my mind on my studies. My only distraction in school was swimming or band.

I tried to make the best of an overall confusing situation. I felt what he was doing was wrong, but wasn't sure what exactly "it" was. Everything that once brought odd and sometimes good sensations had stopped feeling good and arousing; it was replaced with pain. I had learned to focus my mind away from myself.

*What are the coping skills you are using? Are they helpful or harmful?*

*Do you think those coping skills are distractions from facing your truth?*

*"I can travel anywhere in the world on the Astral Plane."*
*~Sher Unbound*

Between the growing sense of the immorality of the situation with Father and a health class discussion of incest one semester, I was convinced someone needed to know what was happening to me. I couldn't tell my sisters, *not* my stepmother, nor any friends. *I felt trapped.* Feelings of shock, shame, and validation returned to me in waves as the days passed. My mind was focused on what had been on the screen in front of the class, the words imprinted in my mind forever. *Sex with family members is incest and it is illegal. Sex with children is wrong.* I repeated that over and over in my head, hearing the teacher's voice like a loudspeaker in my head.

*I was bad* because I allowed myself to like the feel of his touch, of the orgasms, of teasing men with my body and using my sex as leverage. These thoughts circled in my mind, distracting me from my classwork. Would I go to jail? Do they put teens in jail? What would my friends say when they knew how bad I was? Who would ever like me again after this? How was I going to confess to my mom?

Near the end of the school week, my nerves were making me sick. It was nothing new to me; my stomach ached any time my nerves were jump-started. Deciding to go to the office in school to be excused for the day, I went home.

Safe. Let me think, I just need to think. Who could I tell?

While I was home, sitting in my room, I heard heavy footsteps coming down the stairs to the hall where my room was. He called my name out and I froze. I had forgotten to tell the school to call my stepmom at work, not my father. Fuck!

He called my name again and I stopped breathing. I had started the habit of locking my bedroom door, but had not thought ahead that he would figure out I was in my room because the door was locked (I wasn't exactly on top of things then). He was outside my door, knocking…

"Baby doll, you in there?"

Don't breathe. Don't move, Sherri. The knob turned and stopped because it was locked. He knocked again.

"Baby doll, it's Daddy. Are you all right? Let me in, I'll take your temp."

"No, I'm fine, Dad. Just napping. I have stomach cramps again." Maybe that will make him leave, I thought while trying to breathe slowly and quietly as though it would make me invisible, just like a deer does when it's only feet away from the hunter and his gun.

"C'mon Sher, open the door for Daddy. You know it's right to let me in." He tried using his Dad tone.

I got up from the floor, taking what felt like a slow walk of death to the door to unlock it. I moved back to my dresser and stood with my back against it like it was going to protect me. My stomach was churning, and that's when fate smiled. I threw up as he was walking toward me with a smile I once liked and no longer could stomach.

*How do you respond or react when you feel trapped?*

*"I feel the same way a deer does when it freezes just
feet away from the hunter."*
*~Sher Unbound*

After what seemed an eternity of indecision, I made up my mind the following week who I would tell. I didn't like my PE coach, but she was the only teacher with whom my parents were not familiar. Better still, I was one of the girls she chose to ignore, and we both preferred it that way, quiet and out of sight. She was the one who gave us the lessons on Sex Education that semester. Certainly she could be trusted; after all, she did say to tell someone or talk to her if any of us girls had questions or needed to share something with her. I had something to say.

After class one afternoon, I timidly made my request to speak to her. My stomach was turning, and another headache was coming. Following her slowly to the PE office, I held a death grip on my arm full of books and my purse over my shoulder. My mind raced with all kinds of thoughts, mostly: was I doing the right thing?

I had told the truth once before and it had cost me my mother. What would telling gain me? Would someone go to the house and talk to him? Would the whole school know the same way they knew about everything else in people's lives? I was about to share the story about my father and probably get severely punished for that. There was time to change my mind... maybe I could just tell her something stupid like my uniform needed replacing.

We reached her office and I was grateful she chose not to make this any more awkward with small talk. As she placed her clipboard on her desk and hung up her sport coat, I tried to find my voice. Instead, it got a little crackly. I cleared it and started again. I slowly began my story as she kept herself busy with paperwork, not once looking at me. A familiar feeling – being ignored. I started to feel I had made a mistake coming here.

"Do you realize what you are saying?" She finally looked up at me with a grave expression. I felt guilty, as though I had done something horrible. Yes, this was a mistake.

"I know what I am saying and what it means," I replied dryly. "My father had sex with me and has been doing so for years."

She looked at me for a moment, then back at the papers on her desk. "Seems to me you haven't thought this through. First, if what you are saying is true, there's no way to prove your claim. Second, suck it up. You could ruin a man's life with a claim like that. We've all been through this as girls and it's an unpleasant fact."

A mistake. "Well, thanks for the time." I turned around and went to my locker, not sure what I felt.

Shock. Confirmed. Ashamed of being the bad one for even telling someone. It was me that "allowed" him to sexually abuse me, enjoyed it sometimes and had enticed him. Suck it up. This was nothing; it happens to all girls.

I fixed my eyes on all the junk in my locker – a light jacket, books, notebooks, an array of pens. Looking at the picture taped on the inside of the locker door, I paused for a twinge of happiness. I quickly shoved that feeling down as my hand reached for the picture, tearing it off the door and leaving it on the floor. A lie – there was no happiness. That picture was one of the proudest achievements in my life: my band trip to Florida. Nothing else was needed from here or then. "Suck it up," is what she said. I'd do just that.

That night before I ran away, he was snoring slightly. Pushing him off me with a hard shove made him land awkwardly on his knees. This was the first time I ever saw him in that position; weak and confused. Imagination made me wonder if it was shame or guilt, but it was more confusion – like he was snapping to and wondering what he was doing in my room. I'm sure he was drunk because I could smell the alcohol.

He rose to stand, pulling his pants up around his waist, and didn't look at me as he left my room.

After he left my room, I waited for a bit, then quietly began to pack a backpack with a few precious belongings (one being a costume jewelry pin of a sparrow my grandmother gave to me), hiding the pack in my closet. The next evening while my father and my new mom were out, I took what little money I had, stole a gun from his closet, and kissed my baby sister goodbye.

*What prevents you from speaking your truth?*

*"It's a lousy thing to tell someone they matter,*
*without the support to back it up."*
~Sher Unbound

# Four

## Charlie

*"They lie, I lie. Win-Win."*
*~ Sher Unbound*

Locking down any remaining goodness deep inside to protect it, I used my instincts, my youth, and my seductive power for survival as a runaway. I learned sex was a commodity that men were willing to trade in return for housing, rides, food, and money.

To prevent the sting of judgment from others, becoming detached from my emotions was another survival skill to add to my growing list of defenses. Burying my emotions was the only way I could survive what was happening to me.

I hitchhiked to South Carolina, where a young man who I knew from home was stationed. He said he would let me stay with him for a while until he deployed; then I had to stay with other friends. All right, anything was better than the fucked-up mess at home. Sticking out my thumb and doing some walking, my journey began.

On the road, I landed a couple of rides and of course, there was the obligatory sex in trade for a ride. I will give myself credit for being resourceful and somewhat discerning following my instincts over who I hitched a ride with.

"Mr. Obligator," my first ride hitched, was quite aggressive, pounding me into the floor of the forest like he was trying to touch the ground through my spine in some athletic endeavor. I thanked the universe that he came fast. Funny, they all did – and in odd ways. Pull out fast, not pull out, cum on my belly, or point and shoot it at the ground. All of it was odd at that time, not having a clear understanding of men's sexuality or my own.

Another ride took me to his band he was on the road with. We spent the night together, for which he received the standard gratitude, me showing my appreciation for the shower and a decent meal instead of the "snacks" my babysitting money was covering.

More sex, another shower, and getting dressed in what I had in my pack was followed by a request to watch his band play at their gig that evening. The band was a cover band, playing radio favorites. His bandmates weren't too happy to have me there with him; my age was no secret and it didn't occur to me to lie about it – not yet. After their gig was over, he told me they were getting ready to move on to the next show and I was welcome to ride with him. Thanking him, I passed on the offer and we parted company in that town. This was one of the few times there was kindness in people I met.

My next ride landed me with who would be my roommate. He was a surprise because he was not interested in sex for a ride. This man was my ride into the city of Charleston, my intended destination. Cool, good-looking, and more of a conversationalist than me. As fate would have it, we wound up renting a small place together, or rather he rented it and I crashed in return for a few light chores.

He seemed to understand what life was like for me; he never asked for sex, but I felt the need to offer. One night while I was showering, he was using the bathroom sink and I made the offer for him to join me. He thanked me and passed, telling me he believed that I was better than that. He did compliment me on my body and said the offer was tempting, but he wasn't into sex for the sake of having sex.

This was my first experience with a man having values, and a nice break from the fear, adrenaline, and pressure to perform I had lived with. We parted ways when I couldn't find work to help with living expenses, and the work I found did not sit well with a man of standards.

Being underage, I couldn't land "legal" employment in the part of the city I was living in, so… meet "Charlie" (after the perfume I wore), the new girl in town.

*What part of yourself needs the most love?*

*"Why fight to survive when this is all there is?"*
*~ Sher Unbound*

No skills, not of age, what do you do for money? You create your own job, being resourceful and using what you have. I had sensual moves in dancing and was good at moving on the floor. Getting a man's attention was an easy trick; small talk was a snap too. Conversation was easy if I didn't have to talk about myself. *(Fun fact: I still don't like talking about myself.)*

Except for sewing, housework, and babysitting, I possessed no work skills. Too young to waitress (I tried and was fired for false ID) at the places where the real money was, no diploma and well... I knew sex. There was rent to pay for the trailer I had just rented through a "favor," food to buy and clothes. If nothing else, I was resourceful and believed myself to be invincible. Everything would be all right in the end is what I wanted to believe, but feelings of inadequacy and a little loneliness were tapping me on my shoulder.

Through the classifieds, I answered an ad for a model, thinking that I was young and pretty enough to model. I found my way to the office space where the ad said to go for an audition. The building was rundown, and frankly, I'm not sure why I went inside except that I was hungry and desperate.

Finding the office number on the floor plan, I went up the stairs and knocked, though I had no idea why I knocked. I suppose I thought it was good manners. Feelings of anxiety were building when an average, good-looking man opened the door and ushered me in. The hairs on the back of my neck were tingling, alerting me to pay close attention to every detail. He made no request for me to sit down, no small talk of how you are, no introductions.

"Stay there. Stand there a moment." I stopped to stand near where I had entered.

"Turn around." I turned a full circle, stopping to see him scanning me with his eyes up and down my shape.

"I need you to undress." I sucked my breath in.

"Undress?" I replied quietly as my stomach came up to my throat.

"Undress. Strip. Take everything off. I need to see your bush," he said as he lit a cigarette, gesturing to offer me one.

"I'll pass, thanks."

"Suit yourself. Five hundred per shoot. Need to see the bush to make sure you're clean."

"Thanks, I'll pass." I walked out, shaking all the way down the hall and to the street. Air. Breathe. Keep walking. My mind was racing at what I almost walked myself into. My feet hurt from walking in my boots. I needed to find a place to sit. It was hot, I was sweating, and the tears began to roll down my cheeks, one by one.

There are some memories so vivid that in my mind they are as though they happened yesterday. I recall the details because they left such an impact on me in a very present state of mind – they never leave.

Someone was standing over top of me. I was on the ground, semi-slouched against a bench. "You with me? What's your name?" he asked. My head hurt; my stomach hurt. I felt cold.

"I think I am. I just need to sit a moment." I began to pull myself up and he placed his hand on my shoulder, then moved it under my arm, allowing me to use him as a crutch. I sat on the bench, feeling confused and out of place. My head was pounding. What happened?

"What happened? Someone hit me?" I asked finally, looking to see who I was speaking to. I noticed his gun and badge. Plainclothes cop.

"No, I watched you sitting here, and you passed out." He paused a moment and began again. "You on anything?"

"No," I said, my mouth dry. "I'm hungry is all. I haven't eaten in a couple of days. I guess the heat got to me." He wasn't as old as most of the cops.

"Do you want me to drop you someplace? Where do you live?" He squinted and dropped his face a little, indicating he wanted me to look up at him. I've always detested that action. If I wanted eye contact, I'd look at you.

No, I can't let him do that. He'll know I'm a runaway and send me back home. No eye contact, Sherri. Your eyes always give you away. I thought of a lie fast, albeit not a good one.

"I have a place in the Pond area. It is kind of far, but I can walk it." I knew he would question me more and want some details. Age, ID, all the usual. He didn't.

"C'mon. Hop in the front, I'll give you a lift." He walked over to his car and motioned for me to get in.

Shit. I'm stuck now. He called across the top of the car, "I have some leftovers I need to get rid of. Mind if we grab a bite at my place?" Are you serious? Twice today, is this for real? I guess I had gullible or naive written all over me. Thinking quickly, I lied again.

"No, but you can drop me at the park by my place. I'm meeting some friends there before dark." No way was I going to go to his place. Who knows what I'd get myself into. I had already had that experience at home a year before when I accepted an invite to a party. He shrugged his thin shoulders as I dropped my eyes.

"Sure, if you want." He motioned me to an unmarked car, which was very marked. They are obvious: plain rims, bland paint, and always the older-model car.

I climbed in the front seat after he moved some things over, but it didn't look like a cop car inside. No radio, no scanner. Trash on the floorboard in the front. Pricks of my hair were rising again on my neck. My stomach started to hurt. I was either nervous or picking up something that wasn't good.

Small talk. Everyone wants to talk. He spoke, breaking my thoughts, "Where are you from? Your family live around here?"

He had his hand resting on the console, another loosely draped on the steering wheel. I was taking in every detail I could about him. Something told me I needed to.

"No, from the beach area, but I'm staying with friends for the summer." Another lie. Was there anything real about me anymore?

"Is that a fact? What are their names? I know most people around here and I haven't seen you before. No drugs?"

Racing thoughts. "No. I've smoked a little weed, but I'm not on drugs. I am just hungry. Been pretty busy and didn't eat." I wondered how much longer until we reached the park.

"We really can drop by and grab some eats. It's close to the Pond." He moved his hand to my knee and patted it. My skin began to crawl. He gave my knee a quick squeeze and pulled over into a wooded area just beyond a residential zone where I wanted to be dropped off.

"Right here is fine. Thanks," I told him. I was about to reach for the door handle, and he grabbed my hand. It was fast... so extremely fast.

"Whoa, wait up there, missy. You don't think I did this to be nice now did you? I mean to get something for my trouble of picking you up off the sidewalk before some other dude did. I think you owe me."

My head was swirling. Dad all over again. Something for something. Nothing in this world is free. I played stupid. "What are you talking about? Hey, you can take me right back to the place you picked me up. I can walk or take a bus." Another lie. I remembered I could fake sick in a situation like this. I started to hyperventilate on purpose. Make my breathing suddenly rapid so I would pass out but no – that would be the worst thing I could do.

"I mean for you to give me a little blow job. I'm sure you know what that is, a hot little tot like yourself." He pulled his hand away from the steering wheel while he still held the other on my arm. His free hand was rubbing his crotch while he leered at me. "You are a hot little number. I bet you'd be good. Ever blow a cop before?"

I was getting sick and not on purpose. My head was spinning, and I thought maybe I could scream, maybe I could kick and make a noise. There was no one around. We were the only car in that entire wooded area. I could see the houses across the park where I desperately wanted to be. My breath was increasing, and I began to struggle to find my breath.

This sudden change in me must have startled him. "Hey, wait. Whoa... whoa girl! This was a scare. I wasn't gonna make you do anything. This was to scare you! You gotta know there's a lot of fucked up men out there who wouldn't think twice about raping you."

I was crying with short deep spasms, trying to catch my breath, when he let my arm go and put both his hands on the steering wheel. He was looking right through the windshield, almost angry.

I was terrified and trying to catch my breath while he just kept saying, "Breathe; calm down. Just breathe." I was taking breaths as he told me to.

"You okay now?" he asked me, looking at me fully now. It was the first time I let him connect with my eyes. "You've been hurt badly. Nice clothes, good shoes, expensive purse. What's the story?"

I lowered my eyes; they were filled with tears. "You are a jagoff. That was disgusting! I can't tell you. Can I go now? Do you do this to all the girls?" I was angry, frightened, and felt more than confused. I felt like the angry kid that wanted to say all this to my dad and more.

"No, only occasionally a kid will come along that I know I can help, and you seemed like you needed a good scare. What were you doing in that part of town? It's a bad place to be for a nice kid like you." Pausing his conversation, he started the car.

"I was looking for work. I answered an ad and he asked me to strip but I passed." His eyes got wide. "Is that a fact. Do you remember where?" He was back in cop mode. I nodded my head yes and asked for a cigarette. He lit one and passed it to me. I took a deep drag. Exhaling the smoke, I felt an immediate rush of relief.

"I can show you. Here's the address," I said. As I reached for the slip of paper, he asked if anything else happened that made me nervous. I described the story in detail to him while he was driving back to the location.

"Goddamn, you were lucky. Not many come back out of there, not smart enough to turn down the offer." A chill went through me. I remember the feeling I got in that office that told me to run.

We arrived in the parking lot in front of the building. "Is that it?" he motioned while scanning the building with his eyes, looking around for signs of anyone being around.

"Yeah, it's up there." I pointed to the top.

The gear in park, he turned sideways in his seat, looking directly at me. "Look, you'll be in trouble pretty soon if you don't find your way to a fair job. You'll be flat backing or stripping or both. I don't want to see that happen. Let's get you some food, a good night's sleep, and see if we can figure this out tomorrow how to help you." I sensed he was serious.

"Okay. But I won't have sex with you." He sat back in his seat, eyes turned to steel, putting the car into gear to back out and leave.

"No, I won't. Someone already made that fucked up decision with you and I hope to high hell they pay one day."

What? How did he know? I didn't say a word in response. I relaxed once we finally reached his apartment and I made my way to the couch. I was still trying to figure out what he knew about me. Had he spoken to my father? Gone through my purse? Read my diary?

True to his word, he pulled leftovers out in the kitchen and made us a small meal. No TV. No real furniture to speak of. A couch, an ugly orange chair. His kitchen was almost in the living room. His bedroom was close to the living room. Okay. I could sleep on the couch overnight.

"Look, I want you to keep my number in case you need anything. I don't know what I can do to help you, but keep my number if you get in a bind. I'll be there for you." He took a card off his table and, standing a good distance away, handed it to me. I took the card and placed it in my purse.

"Uh, yeah. Thanks. You won't call my parents, will you?"

He looked at me then looked away. "Legally, I must. Morally, I don't think I can. I don't know your story, but it's not a good one. No runaway is this naive and dresses like you do. I'll take the couch and wake you in the morning. The bedroom has a lock on it. You'll sleep better in there."

With that, he took a blanket from his room and stretched out on the couch. I took the bedroom as he said and locked the door.

In a few hours, I was doubled over in cramps and crying. They were painful, almost too painful to get up. Folded over with my hand on my lower abdomen I went to the door and unlocked it, almost yelling. "I'm sick! Something is wrong with me."

He jumped up and asked me several questions. "Maybe go in the bathroom and just sit a few minutes. I'll get you some water."

I went to the bathroom and felt like I had started my period. It wasn't time. In fact, I was late and hadn't really thought of it much. Maybe it was the heat. I dropped my pants. My pants and underpants were soaked in blood. I started to cry and shake at the sight of so much blood.

"No, no! Something is wrong!" I was yelling at him to help me. He came in and stopped at the door, staring.

"You need a doctor. Let's get some clothes. Here's a towel." He handed me one from the rack on the wall.

I wrapped the towel around me and slumped to the floor, my hands pressing in on my abdomen. "I'll be okay. I need to sit." My mind was wild with thoughts. Was I dying? What was all this? I could feel him moving in the room; his silence was disturbing.

"Just let me rest a moment. I'll clean this up. I need a pair of jeans and some pads," I said, eyes closed, ashamed of the mess I was sitting in. I felt dirty. I wanted a shower and some clothes. I needed to leave. How could I leave this embarrassing mess I'd made?

"Look I'm going to call a friend and ask her what to do. I'd rather you see a doctor, but she will know about um, what this is. I have an idea of it." He left the room and I could hear his side of the conversation. "Yeah, there's a lot... Okay... Yeah... Ok. Thanks. I'll explain later."

I woke up to a soft voice asking me to sit up. She was a small lady, with kind eyes and a voice that sounded like southern honey. "What's your name? When was your last period honey? Is the pain bad?" I focused more and thought for a moment. I didn't remember. Before I left home? I knew I hadn't had to worry about pads because I had not had my period in a few months.

"It's been a while. Before I left home. I didn't need to bring..." I stopped. I realized I just confirmed to them I was a runaway. "Please, I can't go home. Please. I can't see a doctor. They'll send me home." She took my hand and helped me up to sit on the edge of the tub.

"No, I don't think you need a doctor, but you will need one if the bleeding hasn't stopped. Let's get you cleaned up and get some fresh clothes." I felt weak, thirsty, and ashamed. The knowledge of what was happening slowly spread through me. I had had a miscarriage.

I showered, changed, and we bagged the clothes to take out to the trash in the alley. I was too ashamed to look up at either of them during any of this. I remained quiet and out of my body. It was moving but my soul was above me watching this entire scene unfold.

She motioned for me to sit next to her on the couch. I walked with my eyes down and sat next to her. "Have you had sex in the past few months? Was there a boy you were running from?" Her voice was like a sedative to my ears. I looked up at her and felt a tear on my cheek.

"Not a boy," I replied with the voice of a mouse. Silence dropped in the room; the weight felt crushing. I'd forgotten the cop was in the room.

"I tried to tell someone, but my teacher didn't listen. So I came to stay with some friends and I have a place but I need money to pay for it and I went to find a job and got scared and have been sick and now I'm here." I was leaving so much out that I'm sure she thought I had lost my mind. She sat still, with compassion and kindness, letting me speak.

I heard the cop cough and was reminded of his presence. I suddenly felt ashamed again. I watched him make a fist while his hand was at his side. He wouldn't look up at either of us.

"I gotta take off. Get her something to eat and I'll check back later." He left the apartment and it was just us girls.

"Honey, I know. You don't have to say any more. I think you had a miscarriage. You know what that is?" Her voice drew me in every time she spoke. I wanted to tell her, but all I could do was move my head to confirm yes and no.

"You can stay here for a day or two but if you stay longer he can get into trouble because you are... how old are you?" She leaned down a little to see my face, which I had lowered at the sound of the cop's voice. I felt shame come back to my face, remembering he was in the room and what he'd heard.

"Almost 16," I whispered, afraid of the other shoe dropping – it always did.

*How did you first tell your story?*

*"It takes courage to speak our truth."*
~ *Sher Unbound*

I needed a job and ventured back out, answering more want ads. Push through, Sher, you need this no matter what.

I went inside and was struck by the smell of cigarettes, alcohol, and sweat. The darkness was hard to adjust my eyes to. There was an exceptionally large-shouldered man behind the bar and one other shorter man sitting opposite him sipping a drink. Both turned to look at me when I entered. The shorter man smiled a toothy grin and stood up, walking over to me. Holding his hand out to take mine, he introduced himself. One hand on my shoulder now, the other still holding mine, he was guiding me toward the bar.

"Come in, have a seat. Can I get you a drink?" Forgetting to give him my name, I sat in a swivel seat and turned sideways to see his face.

"A glass of water, please." I barely said it before it appeared in front of me. The bartender gave me a friendly smile and asked my name. "Charlie." I lied, and they knew it.

They knew the routine well. Young girl, off the road, broken, made up name, no questions asked. Just teach them the ropes and rake in the money. The girls (most of them) survive and everybody is happy, sort of.

I was sensing something not good, but not quite bad either. No danger just yet. "Charlie, that's short for Charlotte?" asked the man next to me.

"Yes. Charlotte is old fashioned; I like Charlie." I was thinking, I'm getting good at this game. They lie, I lie. Win-win.

**Do you listen to your intuition?**

*"Know Your Power."*
*~ Sher Unbound*

I don't offer advice, but I will offer a suggestion. *Walk your own path.*

People will always judge you. They judge what they don't understand, or what they see in themselves and don't like. They judge based on comparisons of themselves to others.

I wasn't ashamed while dancing on the stage, under the spotlight. It was a blessing to not see the men at their tables, only their shadowy figures filtered by the bright stage lights. I was a conduit of the electricity surging in the room. Every step, grind, drop, and turn made me feel it was me who conducted the flow and feel of the room. That was pure energy, pure power. Placing my focus on the beats drowned out my thoughts of disgust knowing I *was* the beat, the music, the electricity. They were watching the untouchable *"Charlie."*

Feel the music; let it wake the "Fire Down Below" and then "Come to Papa." The songs drummed across the room. Close my eyes and feel the pleasure of the beats. The dancing was for me. It was the only way I could take away the images of the men watching me and the thoughts I could hear.

I knew the men watching were responding in the way intended – the more bumps, swishes, and grinds, the more aroused they became. Their arousal was money to me, and to the owner it was a fortune. Charlie was his little "star;" I was his bank. The more seductive she was, the more money the customers spent.

An odd thing though – my real emotions didn't matter. I had learned to paint a facade on my face, a plastered seductive smile complete with cherry lips and a G-string on my ass. My only concern was making money and living another day.

**How do you remove unwanted images from your mind?**

*"Look in the mirror.*
*You'll see me looking back at you."*
*~ Sher Unbound*

There were times when there would be some guilty feelings for seducing the men, especially knowing the only way they would be allowed to speak to me was through the bartender or the owner. There was a status level of protection from the owner and bartender, against the seedy, the lechers, the dirtbags who only wanted to own me.

They both shared with me all I had to do was let either of them know if I wasn't comfortable with the men who were buying me drinks. There was a catch, though – "uncomfortable" meant they weren't allowed to hit me or be abusive physically. Otherwise, it was "just a lap dance" unless they paid in advance for the time in a room across the street.

I didn't have much of a say while I was "on the clock" about who was going to buy me, but the owner did. That was part of the protection. I will give him credit for being a decent enough man to have turned many of them away. And yes, I did have sex with him – the owner. He was one of the few who taught me sex could be "nice."

The bartender was serving me 7-Up and the customers champagne. They thought they were buying me glasses of the bubbly drink for the anticipated happy ending on their part.

All of this was intoxicating to a naive teen – emotionally unprepared, detached, and over-sexed. This was equal to a sense of personal power wielded by my youthful body and my knowledge of how to use it to hypnotize the men watching. This knowledge proved to be valuable to me as a prostitute; however, the stage and my seat at the bar were the boundary lines for the extent of my power.

I left my goodness buried deep inside, disassociated, and climbed out of my body to allow the disgusting touches and thick fat tongues to find their way. Prostitution was money, a way of making a living. I allowed my body to be used by men who wanted to feel, even for a moment, like they had control over someone so young and innocent.

They weren't aware that I wasn't emotionally present. Neither of us held any power or control in those few moments. I was always out of body, far away from them infecting me with their needs. From the moment they laid eyes on me on stage, until they paid me for the pleasure of my company – multiple times in a night – it was me in control of each of them, always holding the power.

*Name all the ways you hold personal power.*

*"I always held the power."*
*~ Sher Unbound*

# Five

## I *Am* a Good Woman

*"How many red flags have to drop before I get it?"*
*~ Sher Unbound*

A little while into this scene, one young man repeated his visits to me almost nightly. As meeting new people goes, he was a friend of the person I was staying with. I wasn't sure about him at the time, and later learned why.

Sadly, I needed to belong to someone – anyone. I wasn't aware at the time I was flirting with him, but it was a pattern that I would repeat several more times in my life. Lacking love, self-love, and self-worth, I sought anyone who would offer me the time of day and allow me to feel some value, even if that value was for sex. He was cute, employed, and it seemed like we could get along.

My usual survival behavior came into play – I made myself have sex with him even though I did not want to. If I was seeking attention, then I should have sex, right?

It wasn't long before I became pregnant by him. We had not spoken of marriage and I think we both planned to just live together until after the baby was born. He was offering me a home and steady income from something other than working on my back or on the stage. It sounded alright at the time. Why not play along?

My pimp, or "Keeper" as I called him, wasn't thrilled about this idea. Less than pleased, he had tried a few tricks to convince me I was making a mistake, including letting me know he could find me and reach me anytime, anywhere.

Before Mr. Keeper or I knew of my being pregnant, he'd picked me up from my place. We were supposed to be going to the club, but that's not where we ended up. He was talking a lot, seemed irritated with me, and revealed he had been having me watched as he leaned toward the glove box. Opening it, he intentionally exposed the gun in the glove box, along with some random junk and some pictures, but I didn't see what the pictures were of.

He closed the glove box and continued his one-sided conversation. Mr. Keeper had also had the place where I was staying with my friends watched and shared more with me than I wanted to know about the young man I was seeing. Where we went next was the end of my relationship with Mr. Keeper and his friends.

He took me to a hotel different from the one I normally went to across the street from the club. When we got into the room, there was a young teen boy there, not much older than I was.

"Make sure she stays put. Keep an eye on her. No phone. Understand?" The boy nodded nervously in agreement. He was thin and almost pale-looking, and it seemed like his whole face sucked in when he took a drag of the cigarette he was smoking. My mind was in flight mode. Something told me I was in trouble.

A little time passed before the kid asked if I wanted something to drink or eat. No. I wasn't hungry. "What's going on?" I asked, fear and concern in my voice.

He looked up at me and said, "All I know is you made him mad. You've been seeing that guy from the club, right?"

"Yeah, so? I'm not owned. I can see who I want, and in fact, I'm quitting," I said with shaky defiance.

He looked right into my eyes, standing within a few feet of me, and took a long draw on his cigarette. "No. You can't. That's what he's mad about. You are his girl, his property. You don't fuck anyone he doesn't know about. You did. And now it has to be handled."

"No. No. I need to get out of here. No." I was almost whispering.

He heard me and walked hard across the floor to a dresser, grabbing what looked like Polaroids. Shoving them at me, he said, "Look! Look, this is what happens when you step out of line." He forced the pictures toward my hand.

I saw the top image. A girl. Just a girl. Face bloody, her naked body with slashes across her breasts and stomach. She looked dead. I felt green inside, like my entire soul was coming up from someplace vile. I turned my head. "No, I don't want to see." I pushed the images away. That's what was in the glove box.

I lit my own cigarette and stood by the door.

"You better not leave. I'll have to hurt you and I don't want to. He'll beat me for that. No one is supposed to ever touch Charlie without permission." His voice trailed off into a quiet, fearful tone.

Thoughts of home came to mind in that moment – my twisted, fucked-up parents. My room, my friends, my family; suddenly I was missing everyone I knew. This wasn't a game anymore. This was real. Someone was going to be hurt because I allowed them to fuck me without paying for it.

Deciding I needed time to think, I spoke up.

"Yeah, I'm hungry. Let's get something to eat. Can we go downstairs?" I was planning to buy time and form a plan.

"I don't know. I can lose my place if I do. I work for him too, you know. You don't want to know." He paused a few moments, lit another cigarette, and said, "Yeah. What the hell. I'll get it for telling you anyway. I don't want to see you get in deeper than you are. You seem like a decent person and you don't belong here." He grabbed a key off the dresser and opened the door.

We ordered a soft drink each and some fries. While we sat there, I looked around for a phone. I spotted a payphone outside on the sidewalk and one in the diner by the kitchen area. "Hey, I need to make a call. Please, you got a quarter to loan me?"

"I'm gonna get beat for this. He'll kill me. You calling home?" I wondered how he guessed that I was missing home.

"No, I can't go home," I replied, lowering my eyes, recalling the last time I was home. My sister. I wondered how she was. I missed her.

He slid a quarter across the table to me and I got up, pulling HIS number from my purse like he said to. He said to call if I needed help.

I dialed the numbers; it rang a few times. I was about to hang up before a man's voice answered with a groggy, "Hello?"

"Hey, it's Charlie. I need your help. I'm in trouble."

*Write about the person in your life you want to thank.*

*"I believe there are Angels that walk among us*
*who are just as damaged as I am."*
~ *Sher Unbound*

I was pregnant at 17 years old with no idea how to take care of the growing baby inside me. I had no access to anything other than a phone in the hall of the apartment building we lived in. Our transportation was a cab or walking and most times that was only done with him escorting me.

With no clue as to what was really happening to my body, looking back on this time, it's a miracle my first-born ever made it into the world. I didn't want to appear ignorant, but I asked so many questions of friends and a few nurses and managed to read a few magazine articles on pregnancy. My health could have been better; I put on more weight than I ought to have, my breasts hurt all the time and my body felt miserable. The water weight was threatening me with toxemia.

The military dependent's ID was my ticket to my OB appointments at the local Naval Hospital. The OB at the Naval Hospital was hard to be around, and I felt condemned every time I had an appointment with him. He never had a kind comment for me, but would always tell me I had no business being pregnant at my age; what was I planning to do to raise the baby? He'd ask me things like where was my brain? What was I going to do for my education? I never felt more discouraged than at those visits. It took days to shake off the sting of his words after each visit. Those questions chipped away at my already low self-esteem.

My knowledge of the female body was severely limited to sex and menstruation. What I knew of children was less. There was the knowledge I had gained from babysitting and helping raise my baby sister: kids always needed to be fed, changed, and attended (watched). That was my wealth of knowledge about kids and homemaking. I knew how to clean the apartment but I barely knew how to do laundry or grocery shop. Children are not meant to have babies nor raise children.

Home had not crossed my mind in a while, but it didn't matter. I was only missing a few people there. I was "established" with an address, going to be a mom, and living in a decent apartment with some nice neighbors. I was making friends in the building and living a better life. It was not the best, but it wasn't the streets or flat-backing either.

Speaking of which, Mr. Keeper, my pimp, had located the common number used in the building we rented an apartment in. He called me one day to check on me. It wasn't odd to me then, but as I look back on it, he really was either concerned for my well-being or looking to have me return to him. It's nice to think he was genuinely concerned.

At midday, there was a knock on the apartment door. I cheerfully answered with a smile and hello, but the person at the door was not someone I expected. My heart raced from calm to feeling it might explode in my chest in the blink of an eye. My stomach was in my throat already and I could feel my muscles tense. He let the words roll off his tongue.

"Hello. How's Daddy's Girl?"

*How many times have you tried to find freedom? How does one break free?*

*"I'm not your girl."*
*~ Sher Unbound*

My stomach was in shreds, my nerves felt on fire. My skin was crawling. Feeling I had no choice but to let him inside, I moved back from the door and left it hanging open. He stepped in and closed the door. The click of the door made me jump a little. He looked around and took a seat at the kitchen table. Panic filled my insides, causing every hair on the back of my neck to stand up. My stomach hurt and I was holding it, making my swollen belly more pronounced.

"How did you find me?" I asked in my best adult voice. I wouldn't look at him. I lost my manners and offered no water or drinks. Moving to my usual spot at the small kitchen table, I sat down and lit a cigarette.

"How far along are you?" he asked me, and then said something about my boyfriend. His words were only a buzz in my ears.

"How did you find me?" I asked again, letting the cigarette burn between my fingers, nervously flicking the ashes as though the cherry-red tip had to be clean.

"I have a few friends that owed me some favors. You weren't hard to find. Are you seeing a doctor? You know you can come home and we can take care of this." He placed his hand close to mine and I pulled it away.

"I can't. I have things here. It wouldn't be a good idea." I still was not looking at him.

"I need to speak to your, er, boyfriend. What are his intentions? Are you planning on marrying him?"

"No. We had not talked about that, but I don't want to marry. I'm too young and I'm not that fond of him." I snubbed my cigarette out in the now perfectly arranged ashes in the ashtray.

He spoke to me like he was talking to a child not a woman.

"Baby girl, you do have options. You don't have to do this. If you don't come home, then…" – blah, blah, blah was all I heard.

He sat there, waiting for me to answer. I knew he knew the answer. He always asked me questions he knew the answer to. "You have options, but they are limited. I'll be back after dinner tonight and he and I are going to have a talk." As he finished, he stood and pushed his chair in, military-style as always.

I couldn't think of anything to say but, "Okay, Daddy" as I had always done. Obedient. The good girl.

*If you can't trust yourself, how can you hope to stand by your beliefs or boundaries?*

*"If you love me then let me go."*
*~ Sher Unbound*

He returned that same evening. Each word that was said was like a knife in my stomach. He sat across the table from my boyfriend, who was an enlisted service member. I remember looking at my boyfriend and thinking, "I don't love him. I don't want this."

*Red Flag #1: The man who I was calling my "boyfriend" terrified me. The first time he lost his temper was when I was tired of all his drinking and falling down drunk at night, so I dumped a six-pack of beer down the kitchen sink. First mistake – never take away an alcoholic's poison of choice until he or she is ready to give it up OR you have people to help you. The first rule of living with him I remembered was to never touch his alcohol or talk about his drinking. He hit the side of the refrigerator so hard that night where I was standing, he rocked the unit sideways.*

Father was telling him the options for the situation we were in. I glanced over at my boyfriend – was he even a boyfriend? He was not someone I was in love with, that much was certain. I looked at him several times, at his chain-smoking (not noting my own), his foot bouncing his leg at a rapid, steady pace like he had to pee or something.

Two men I didn't care for... sitting directly across from each other. The talk was quite formal in tone.

"You realize I could have you thrown in the brig for statutory rape? She's underage. You are 21, 22, son? Do you plan to take care of your responsibility and marry her, or do you face time?"

At this point, I remember wishing I had stayed with Mr. Keeper. Everything was black and white with him. This was in no way how I visualized my future.

My heart was tearing in two. I had no desire to marry this man, no desire to return home, no idea of who I was or what I wanted to do. All I knew was we created this child and it was my responsibility to do my best to take care of the baby and myself. That was the extent of the knowledge of my purpose.

My baby's father spoke finally. "Sir, I see what you are saying, and I have to live up to my word. I'll marry her as soon as I can take leave." He took a long swig of his beer and crushed out his cigarette in an almost final stamp of his honor and word. His shoulders were slumped somewhat – was he feeling defeated like I was? Was he feeling cornered too? The room began to spin from all the cigarettes I'd smoked. I excused myself to wash my face, leaving them both sitting in silence as if the other was not present.

"Baby girl, I need your answer. Are you accepting his honor, or do you go home tonight with me?" I froze.

We all knew there was no returning home, as well as we knew that this was not the best solution for any of us. It was a power play for control once again – the control my father lost when I ran away from home.

In that moment, we both knew we had to deny our own soul to "do the right thing," to survive this mess. Neither of us wanted to be married but we knew it was the only alternative.

*I wanted to say you have no control over me. I am 17 and can do as I fucking well want to do. You controlled me for too long. You used me for your pleasure instead of being a man and seeking your wife – your own flesh-and-blood daughter. You bastard. You bastard... I was your sex doll. I was your crowning achievement in your life. Are you proud of how I turned out? Pregnant and you can't do a fucking thing about it. How's it feel to be powerless?*

I didn't say that. I heard it in my head and bit my tongue, swallowed the words with the bile I felt building in my throat. All that came out was the meager, "Okay. Yeah. I guess." I felt so powerless.

It made me ill to see that man who was biologically my father. The one I only wanted to love me as most men would love and revere their daughters. The man who I thought was supposed to protect me. The man who was two different men in one body, creating so much confusion and anger in me.

*Is it wiser to make a bad choice or no choice at all?*

*"There are three options when you find yourself cornered with ignorance: Learn, Run, or Exist."*
~*Sher Unbound*

We married in a civil ceremony at my parents' home. All his truth came out on the bus ride to my parents' home and on the day of the wedding, and it was let out even more after.

The bus was stuffy, smoky, and hot. No windows would open and the bathroom was bad enough that I made myself, at five months pregnant, wait for each stop to use the restroom. All I could think of was how nauseous and resistant to all this I felt. I was as resistant as a child being told to lay still and accept it in the dark of their room.

I barely ate and knew if I drank water, there would be no holding my already fragile bladder.

We only spoke when we needed to – pretty much like the rest of the marriage – choosing to read and nap the entire ride.

This wasn't the wedding or the man I dreamed of marrying as a little girl. My dreams were of a wedding on the beach near my beloved ocean. My dress would be a long and flowing boho dress in a pastel color, and my groom would adore me. The happy bride who was whisked away from the wedding with joy and anticipation of the future. Where was the music, the laughter, the kisses, the love?

It would be all right, I told myself. Always do your best and never let him know how you really feel. Feelings don't matter, remember? Your feelings about this are not important.

My new mother made my dress for me. It didn't take her long to put one together that fit my oversized hips and belly. There were simple decorations and a nice cake, and of course the full meal for our guests. Nothing looked appetizing to me – only sleep.

One odd note is still interesting to this day: we weren't quartered in my old bedroom. It was locked and we slept in my brother's old room, now a guest room.

My new mom still wasn't happy with me, but was as gracious as she could possibly be. She didn't ask much about the pregnancy but did give a few of the usual jabs about my weight; those jabs would never change. During preparations for the wedding, one stop was at the courthouse to obtain written permission to marry because I was underage and to sign the marriage license.

How ironic is that? My parents were there to give me permission to marry someone I didn't want to marry in the first place.

*In what ways have you given up your personal power?*

*"Explain to me why I need your permission to make
my own decisions?"*
*~ Sher Unbound*

I guess at this point, he was my official fiancé for a few hours. Congratulations to me.

A few friends of my parents arrived on a Saturday, and one guest was the boy I had a genuine crush on for-ev-er. I felt compelled to give him the usual, "Oh, I'm terrifically happy! I can't wait to start my new life." I felt guilty for lying to him. We got on with the civil ceremony, gratuitous pictures, cutting the cake with a military ceremony, and that was that.

I felt trapped, and wanting to run away again was my only thought of happiness.

*Red Flag #2: Hours after we said "I do," my new husband was busy making sexual advances to my friends that day.*

My prison was closing in around me. I was tired; I only wanted to sleep. That wasn't about to happen as I was now "owned."

*Red Flag #3: My husband raped me that night, the first of many times over the course of almost ten years. I was property. Not of legal age, I was a child bride and would follow as I was told to do.*

At this very moment of writing this, I can offer him compassion and understanding for the next ten years that followed. This is a conflicted feeling and thought, I won't lie to you on that. It's one of those things that to resolve it, I must understand what he was going through as well.

He was reacting to the stories he grew up with and relating them to his current situation. He was as trapped as I was. We had not wanted to marry. He wanted to do the right thing and help me during my pregnancy, possibly with plans for the child and me after the baby was born. Neither of us wanted the next ten years of rage, pain, sexual abuse, or the damaged children we would create for the world ahead.

*Red Flag #4: On the way home from the wedding ceremony, he became agitated. I suspect now it was because he had gone without a beer for a full day. Whatever it was, I don't recall. I recall his anger with either me or the situation.*

As we were unloading from the bus, it was hot and we had several blocks to walk ahead of us with no money for a cab. I carried what I could, and he was carrying a few suitcases and wrangling the sewing machine my new mother had gifted to me. He became overheated and enraged at everything. I think it was his way of saying how angry he was at all of it. He threw the sewing machine, weighing more than 25 pounds, across part of the piping hot tar parking lot we were left in. There were tears in my eyes and no words to speak while this first scene of many to come played out before me.

My belly was full at 5 months pregnant. I was hot, with swollen legs, and he was throwing a sewing machine? It was frightening and shocking watching this display. The machine wasn't damaged much and I managed to carry it myself on the walk home along with my bag. We didn't say a word to each other the rest of the day.

*Red Flag #5: I didn't know him. I knew of him. I knew only what he chose to share. I knew what his father and other family members shared. He had led a tortured life, as I had. It didn't connect then that we ought never to have been together, but it was the lot we chose, and I chose to tough it out the best I could. I was taught, "You made your bed, you lie in it." So, I did. Every time he said so.*

We never ought to have been married or had children, but we had four children together in our nine years of marriage.

During those nine years, I did a good job of keeping the house immaculate, learning to cook and how to do laundry, but I sucked at the budget (I never learned budgeting from my parents or school) and actually, I believed he was represented well in public. There were a few friends that lived in the base housing complexes where we lived, and I was grateful for the distractions of their company.

Again, it was beneficial to lean on the community; I learned from the ladies in the complex everything possible about what makes a good marriage, how to raise my kids, and how to not mess with his private life. I believed if only I did well in one thing, any one thing, he wouldn't hate me as much as he did. I held the belief this was all my fault. Our life, his anger, his drinking, his beating us... all of this was my fault.

*Red Flag #6: He was an alcoholic like his father and other family members. Alcohol made him mean, extra mean. When he didn't have it, he was even more mean. The worst beatings were when we lived overseas, isolated and with no help.*

The truth was it never mattered how clean the house was, how much weight was lost, how many times his favorite dinner was made or whether I joined him in drinking and partying. It didn't matter how many times I lay there while he helped himself to my body in any way he chose. There was never any mind paid to how many times his urine was cleaned up from places he'd drunkenly empty his bladder in the apartment. None of it mattered. We were all paying the price of his pain and shame by being his punching bags and sex toys – including the children.

What mattered was detaching. I learned that skill as a teen years before. I could have erased him from my mind as though he wasn't there. When he was finished with me, I'd clean up and the next day begin the process of salvaging what little was left of my dignity. The memories are still there; my children's voices are as well, asking me for help.

**How many red flags do we need to know it's time to get out?**

*"I was never a bad mom. I was unaware
there was a choice."*
*~ Sher Unbound*

It was hard work to move beyond the shame I carried in believing I did not protect my children while they were being abused. Some images will never be unseen, and some come without warning. They are like some mysterious part of my brain with a lock on it.

One memory is especially hard for me to write, although this is a good exercise for the processing and release of feelings. We lived overseas in a hot, tropical location. We had two children at that time, both boys. We were invited to a barbecue at someone's home and he was in an especially foul mood about something. It doesn't matter; what came next does.

On the way there, my oldest son was still crying from the spanking he received just before we left the housing unit, setting off the baby's crying. Crying grated my ex-husband's nerves hard. He kept telling them to shut up, turning up the music on the radio to drown them out, and would not pull over to let me see what the problem was. The loud music was making the baby cry harder, creating a scene of madness in the car. Each time I tried to place my arm over the seat to try and soothe the boys, he would crack his elbow across my arm, leaving what felt like a charlie horse.

We arrived at the barbecue, and as I was walking around to the back of the car, he stepped in front of me and said, "They stay in the car." He stood there glaring at me. I was horrified. It was over 100 degrees in the baking sun, and I knew they could not be left in the car.

"No! Are you crazy? They'll suffocate in there!" I said in a loud whisper.

He stood firm in front of me with his fist doubled up. There were people in the yard watching this scene. My oldest was pressing his tiny hands against the glass of the backseat window and crying; his face was beet red and sweat was covering his head, little snot bubbles forming at his nostrils. I knew they were already overheating.

I screamed at him, "Let me get them out!"

He grabbed my arm and squeezed hard enough to make me think he would break it, warning me not to embarrass him in front of his Commanding Officer. I stood, frozen, not caring about my arm. My mind was racing, my heart knowing they desperately had to get out. If I tried, I'd pay. I made my move by dropping and twisting at the same time. I went for the door handle and got to it. He grabbed my hand with a force that felt like a hammer. I didn't care; I was frantic to get them out, they would die in the heat.

When he grabbed my hand, a woman walked over and laid her hand on his arm while saying, "C'mon, let's go have a beer! Sherri, grab the kids and take them in. My, it sure is hot out here!"

He didn't have a choice but to go with her because her husband was his CO. She knew what was happening, as she was also being victimized by her husband. I bless her every time she crosses my mind, which has been frequently since then. She saved two babies that day, but sadly, I was certain she received her punishment the same as I did mine later that night. It didn't matter, the kids were alive another day.

Other memories are haunting as well, such as the sexual abuse during his drunken rages. I lost track of how many times he raped me. While the images don't hurt as they once did, the pictures are still there.

My oldest tried to intervene as a child to protect his brother. He took a lot of the punishment through sexual abuse, beatings, and verbal abuse so his little brother would not be hurt. Thousands of tears were cried, and I still hear my ex calling him "retard" and "dumbass" when he was less than two years old. I took as much of the beatings and verbal abuse as I could by distracting him or offering myself as the target instead of the children. Those times the pain was worse both emotionally and physically.

I tried to block him out, close my eyes, think of other places or things, but his penetration was forceful. My nails ripped at the sheets trying to place the pain anywhere in my body but my mind. One day I learned if I left my body, disassociated from myself and the scene, his efforts to humiliate me were not as effective. When he grew bored of me, he would turn his attention to the children again, humiliating them. It was at these times that fake crying in pain to keep his attention was the game that had to be played. Other times, it was inevitable we all were beaten and could only cry together in the end while he was passed out.

The self-punishment for not knowing about my own children being sexually abused took over half of my life to stop. Eating disorders were out of control most of my life. I tried to cry, but most times the tears weren't there. I tried praying, prescriptions (Ativan and Hydrocodone) to numb physical pain, alcohol, smoking, using marijuana, and attempts at taking my life to ease the pain of memories playing like a bad movie.

Much later, it was a lesson for me to see how my attempts to over-protect were harmful to the children as well. There are times when I attempted to share with them our frightful history to help them understand this is not what life ought to be. Attempts to protect them from the world I was trying to escape only made it worse for their behavior and emotions. They know the full story now, each recovering from their painful past. My heart has never been prouder of them than to watch them rise above and grow beyond their deep and painful past.

Near the end of our marriage, my feeling of strength in myself as a woman began to increase. Making plans to leave with the kids was my priority, but I knew that we would need help. Educating myself was going to be my ticket out.

My plan was to secretly go about asking questions, making phone calls during the day while he was at work to whatever agencies I could at the time, and placing calls to AA, NA, and social services at one point. The worst place to call (then) was social services. They separated the kids and me – placing them in foster care and me in a women's shelter "for safety." Children were not allowed to stay in women's shelters at that time. I'm grateful for the movements and progress our society has made – but it was not helpful then. That entire experience led me to believe staying in the abusive situation was our only option.

I can feel empathy for him in some ways – we were the weights around his neck, the end to his personal dreams, which he never shared. However, being unaware of boundaries, he knew right from wrong – that never excused his violent actions toward me or his children. Being able to understand why he was who he was was not an excuse for what he did. Violence is violence and there is nothing that excuses child abuse, rape or beating anyone.

*What darkness in you are you afraid to look at and offer yourself compassion for?*

*"The prettiest eyes have cried the most."*
*~ Unknown*

A day came that silenced my voice and I lost what humanity I had gained with my plans to leave. He was either buying drugs or paying back a debt and gave me to a man in a parking lot at a bar. As a married woman, I was having sex in the back of an old El Camino with some stranger for a debt that was not mine to pay.

All the classic signs were there of love bombing, the excessive and public apologies, but I knew better than to embarrass him in front of anyone, even when alone. Despite all my emotional numbing, disassociation, and unemotional availability to everyone, a smile and pleasant manner were plastered on my face as though the world was perfect.

The neighbors could hear our pleading cries for him to stop hurting us, but I was persistent in fronting that all was good and well. I kept a smile on when everything inside of me wanted to cry while I was accepting his grand "loving gestures" of apology gifts he would present to me in front of my friends by making a big show of the gift.

He always made things look good in front of his friends, but toward the end he became sloppy. He would show his temper toward me in front of people, but not many would step in and say anything – his temper was wicked enough no one questioned him. Sometimes they would ask me in a quick moment if I was alright. My answer was always a coldly polite, "Yes. Thank you." The same voice that people hear from me today when I am not all right.

This was my life for ten years, protecting the children to the best of my ability, but that was never enough for my mind. The guilt was consuming me, creating anxiety and depression, and my eating disorder was out of control. Weight gains and losses of 100 pounds at a time were a regular occurrence for me, creating an eating disorder that is still present today but under control.

Our normal was chaos and pain. On several occasions, I tried to escape, but each time he found us, and the punishment was severe. At one point, he held a knife to my oldest son's throat while he held him like a rag doll, demanding I leave the hotel and return to the apartment with him. I knew that was the last time to ever try and leave without divine help.

It was an act of divine intervention for the apartment to be gutted by flames one day. It was our chance to escape and never look back. No, I didn't set the fire – although it had occurred to me to burn him in the bed (much the same as in the movie with Farah Fawcett – The Burning Bed). He woke up from a drunken sleep one night on the couch and caught the end of the movie.

He looked me directly in my eyes and said, "Don't get any ideas," as his closed fist landed against the side of my head.

"Too late, they were already there." I didn't wake up until the next morning after that comment.

***At what point do you say enough?***

*"When normal is chaos and pain,*
*peace is traumatic."*
*~ Sher Unbound*

What do you do when it seems like it never gets better? You look up. There's nowhere to go from the bottom but up or stay the same.

We were assigned a new apartment in the military housing complex because our family size grew. We had four children now; my youngest was still an infant. All the units were aging and were notorious for the cockroaches and electrical fires.

While I was studying pieces of a quilt in progress, my son ran into the room trying to tell me something, but he was so animated it was hard to understand him. He ran back down the hall and I could see him from my seat. When I looked up at him running back toward me again, this time I saw it following him above his head. A cloud of thick black smoke was crawling across the ceiling toward me. The fire alarms had not gone off.

I was frozen for a moment in time; then my thoughts suddenly snapped to. Grabbing him and our dog, I put them out the front door into the foyer, called the fire department, and ran to find my daughter, who was last known to be in her crib.

The smoke was choking me. I tried again, pulling my shirt over my mouth to breathe. Where was she? I could see her crib was empty and raced out to the back to see if I could see her from the window. Flames were licking the glass and I heard the sirens in front. A fireman called to me to move back and I only remember screaming my daughter was inside still. The glass to the bedroom broke about then.

I could hear sounds of my voice screaming, my ears ringing, and coughing. Nothing could describe the sheer panic of not knowing where my baby was.

I saw a fireman carrying a bundle of blankets and could see the top of her head. Leaving my son standing where he was in the yard, I ran to grab her.

"No, hold on. She's fine. Just needs a little air is all," he said while he walked to the back of the ambulance. Another person was holding my son's hand. It was my upstairs neighbor; her husband had their twins in his arms.

In a few seconds, my daughter was breathing and crying while someone handed her to me, asking if I was okay and other questions.

"Where was she? She was in her crib before the fire..."

A man answered he found her in the bedroom closet in a corner. Apparently, my son put her in there when the fire started. He saved her life.

I went back after a day to survey the damage and see if there was anything to salvage. Nothing. The fish in the tank were dead; everything was charred. The only thing moving were the cockroaches and the sound of my heart beating so loud I felt deaf. The police report showed the fire began in an outlet suspected of shorting out from a junction, with sparks setting the bed next to it on fire. My son had placed his baby sister in the closet for her safety while he came to get me.

Our dog was pregnant at that time and had gone into labor from the shock of the commotion. She gave birth to a litter of 10 pups upstairs in my neighbor's apartment. Graciously, they let her stay a few days while I planned to have her moved to our temporary home.

I tried to salvage makeup, clothes, toys, but everything was permeated with the smoke from the fire. Everything was lost, but not my children and our dog. Honestly, looking back it surprises me because there was the option of giving up. Instead of giving up, unfortunately there were more poor choices made based on what were my *only* options.

My husband was out to sea during the fire, and when sent a message, his response was expected – not a positive one. The man

I met from my neighbors upstairs was out to sea at the time as well, so no help there, although he did lend me the use of his car before he left to sea; there was that for help.

We were offered a temporary stay with my cousin on the other side of the city. I was grateful for the space and the help, though I wasn't quite sure how I would get out of that, except to push through like we always did. It was a small two-bedroom home, where the four children and I had one room, she and her son another. We were uncomfortable, but grateful.

There are always options, but I wasn't to the point of recognizing them clearly. There was the man I was seeing that I met at a party before the fire, the one who was letting me use his car. I still felt like we were "just friends." He wanted the same thing every man wanted from me – to own me, to control me. I wanted freedom and began to wonder if I could gain my independence.

With no skills and no idea of what I wanted to do or how we would survive, the thought of prostitution crossed my mind. It wasn't an option when I looked at my children. I didn't want to be that mother who people judged for their choice of career. Erasing that thought, my search focused on something that would not bring feelings of shame when the children were asked what my job is.

Personally, I have nothing against prostitution. I know why people choose that work. It's not for satisfaction in sex, by far. You make good money and if done right, you can be set for early retirement and somewhat protected. Does the term 'sugar babies' ring a bell? It should; it's the new "legal" prostitution without Mr. Keeper.

*How do you plan, set a goal, or make decisions under deep stress?*

*"Why is it 'friends' is never an option?*
*Does it have to be all or nothing?"*
*~ Sher Unbound*

# Six

## David

*"There is love and then there is the love of an*
*Angel living among us."*
*~ Sher Unbound*

Grateful for the business of the fire being settled, we worked hard to make a life for ourselves. We were able to breathe and think, with no fear of anyone hurting us. Divorce proceedings were underway, and I was free to visit my friends. Then, I met him. My best friend, the man who was my mirror of who I could be.

Since the man I was casually seeing was out to sea, I was grateful for the ability to make my own decisions. I loved it when the guys were deployed, because our circle of friends was usually women and the kids, a strong community of like minds and supportive sisters. We could breathe.

Some memories bring a faint smile to my heart, like the thought of how hard "he" tried to get me to talk to him, and finally asked me to dance instead. I felt flattered, a little curious, and very taken by his boy-like charm. Deciding he'd had enough torture; I accepted his offer.

Between stepping on each other's toes for lack of space, we eventually found a couple of chairs and talked through the early hours of the morning. It felt good to have honest attention paid to me, in a polite and unassuming manner. By my standards, it wasn't a good idea to be flirting, dancing, or dating during a divorce, but I needed his company for some reason. Something told me to pay attention to this.

His energy was high, his laugh too silly for words, and his voice honestly seemed like it never left puberty, crackling and pitching. He was too sweet to ignore, giving me no reason to think of doing so.

**Soul connections happen all the time. Do we recognize them?**

*"Every now and then we meet ourselves in the person
standing in front of us."*
*~ Sher Unbound*

Outings with him were magical. Long summer days at the beach, bonfires at night. We held deep discussions over my current situation, and telling my story provided a much-needed outlet and view into my inner strengths.

I felt confident and capable of anything. Finding my feminine side was fun. I began to wear more dresses and heels, fix my hair more, and match my jewelry. I felt pretty for the first time since dancing at the club. All the things my old self denied me. Date nights were spent out with mutual friends dancing until 2 AM.

There was a dance one night I will never forget. The song "Lady in Red" was playing. He asked me to dance and neither of us looked at each other. We didn't have to. It was a magical moment when silence was prescribed.

My kids adored his playful nature and smile. He played with them and showed me how to do the same. He taught us all to be kids again. My being a few years older didn't matter to him. He only cared that we were happy, healthy, and being the best version of ourselves we could be. He cared about our friendship. David was my best friend.

Sex was never a part of this relationship. Come to think of it, neither of us saw our relationship in that way. He was the first man to ever see me as the woman I am. We kissed only quick little pecks hello and goodbye, and would hold hands on occasion, but it wasn't romance. His hugs were deep and made me feel like everything was well in the world. We enjoyed each other's jokes, stories, and time together and held a common vision for living in the moment.

***What is your vision of a healthy relationship?***

*"Love is when you love the friend in yourself."*
~ *Sher Unbound*

The Universe has a way of placing people in your life, then taking them from you just as fast. A little while after we started hanging out more frequently, he received word he would be deploying too.

David was deployed on West Pac and one day his letters stopped. We had been writing regularly. I always looked forward to his letters that always held amazing insight, and I would share with him my workday and how the kids were doing. I had no desire to see anyone else, not even the man I was seeing before I met David.

*The other day, on Christmas, while sorting through old family pictures, I came across all those he took of the kids and a few of me while we were with friends at the beach. I looked a little closer; not one photo of him. There's one of just his legs – but all others were taken by him behind the lens. I found it interesting he never wanted to be photographed.*

I sometimes wonder if the letters stopped for the same reason he came into my life. It was his time to "Angel" another person who needed his insights. I like to think that is why they stopped, not the manipulation of the man I was dating off and on.

Many times, I wonder where he is now, and how he has been all these years. Does he have a family that loves him as much as he loves them? He had to be an angel walking the Earth, carrying a lesson in love. He breathed a whisper of hope into my life at one of the most uncertain points. I've secretly fantasized over the years that he has tracked me and is still watching my progress and cheering me on.

David, thank you for showing me I am enough and more!

**Have you met an Angel in your life?**

*"Until we meet ourselves, we don't know the depth of Love."*
~ *Sher Unbound*

Once we become aware of love, have been held by its warm embrace, we never forget, and love never lets go. Love finds us in the most peculiar ways. Sometimes it shows us its meaning in day-to-day life – a smile from a stranger, a song, or in the still of a starlit night under the milky way. Sometimes it finds us unaware in the most casual of places. Love finds us when we aren't expecting it to visit.

Once we realize what this chance meeting meant to us, we know deep in our soul: unconditional love never leaves. It's in every breath we take, the way we hold space for others and ourselves, the kind word that brushes away a salty tear, the way we offer compassion and understanding to ourselves and others.

David, I didn't know I loved you unconditionally until after we parted. You knew I was unfamiliar with your love, or any love; you also knew I was not taking our friendship for granted.

You knew of my being unaware, and you shared with me all the good things about life and being free, because you were the embodiment of love. What I did take for granted, or I thought later, was that you were always going to be there.

I have carried regret for long enough for not speaking my heart to you. I know now that this was not a romantic love; what we shared was deeper. It was a soul connection. Once I realized you stepped into my path for a specific reason, that regret was dissolved.

Every word, gesture, and touch mirrored what you saw in me. Your playfulness, corny jokes, deep conversations, cocky smile, and quiet moods all captured my attention. You could have said how you felt in words, but that was not your purpose.

Your purpose was to show me my worth as a woman. To be my mirror. To share with me a rare glimpse of unconditional love that I deserve and didn't find until years later. I met a rare man who honored my very existence and only asked that I do the same – find my worth, live my worth as a woman, and grow with unconditional love.

*Write about a time you found a soul connection in someone.*

*"I know he wasn't a lost love.*
*He was an Angel when I needed one most."*
*~ Sher Unbound*

# Seven

## Learned Behaviors – Not love

*"My good was not good enough."*
*~ Sher Unbound*

During one of our long talks, David had brought up the topic of me continuing my education and finding a job to support myself and the kids. He knew of my intelligence and knew I was an eager learner.

Was a better life reachable? Did I have it in me? Was I capable of making a better life for myself and my children? I felt so capable around him, I knew I could be strong again on my own.

*A bit of a side note here. As of this edit, I am facing another life transition and read my question at the bottom of this letter, "Worry produces nothing. Actions create solutions." that was written a few months back during the beginning of the first draft. How odd it seems that I have been in transition for some time now. Acceptance is an odd concept but a vital one. It's an ongoing process...*

After some wrestling with my thoughts, I took the leap and enrolled in a school for paralegal studies. I excelled in school and graduated quickly through the courses. Unfortunately, I found though I was young, it wasn't easy going to school, battling depression and anxiety, and raising four emotionally troubled children. It made working full-time a challenge, so I had to give in an area and take part-time as a temp for a short while.

I had time with the kids at the beach, David and I wrote letters to one another, and I tried to write a letter to the man I did not choose. That was a hard fail. I sent it and his response frightened me. His anger felt like a betrayal against the calm manner of my best friend, David.

Between the kids and me, we all had our share of emotional struggles after the divorce, the fire, and missing David while trying to sort out who we were as a family with no real place to call home. We survived on looking to the future and sadly, I gave in to an offer from the man I was casually dating. I abandoned myself, putting my desire for freedom aside to make others happy.

**In what ways have you abandoned yourself?**

*"Worry produces nothing. Actions create solutions."*
*~ Sher Unbound*

*"I was born with a purpose.*
*Finding it is my journey."*
*~ Sher Unbound*

*A dear friend recently reminded me that what occurred in my past was the best I could do with the tools available to me at the time. So true, my friend; so true. Thank you. As I move along this timeline of my life, my past feels better each time I read it. The feelings are present, but they pass through, just as was intended with writing to you. Patterns are surfacing that were forming with the ability to recognize them. There is a method to this madness of journaling. ~ Sher Unbound*

Dating was not successful and was based on no boundaries or standards. One of those dates I stayed with for nine more years. He was the one I chose when I felt backed into a corner by his anger. This journey has allowed me to see now how depressed I was through my behaviors and how much I mistreated myself. *I was slipping back into old patterns and beliefs* that David and I had worked out in our conversations. I was doing all I could to not think of him and focus on what my kids needed. They needed a home and I thought they needed a father figure. I thought I needed someone, though what I genuinely wanted was freedom to be me.

For me, life isn't as static as we may think. I believe it is in constant motion, fluid, and moves in all directions. What else could explain all the different paths my life took?

Not hearing from David convinced me it was for the best that we had not stayed connected – or I tried to tell myself that. Did he know I had gone back to school and was working a real job?

Once school was completed, I accepted a temp position as a paralegal in a local firm. It wasn't where I wanted to be, as I now know, but it was a good, steady job with a wage on which I could support myself and four children. I had become complacent and thought the worst was over until I saw familiar behavior patterns developing in my children: lying, stealing, outbursts, and being abusive toward one another. These were the same behaviors their biological father showed us many, many times while I was with him.

Their behaviors were severe enough that a degree wasn't required to know we needed help, which led me to seek out the first of many counselors. Sharing my life with others wasn't easy. It also wasn't helping; they were only being given overviews and broad descriptions of our lives. Talking about the details was beyond challenging, especially while detached from my feelings. Though counseling was helpful, this was not the key to what the kids and I needed. The connection was not quite made because we were lacking in one important emotion – love.

Counseling wasn't effective for them; treatment wasn't effective either. We were all little robots carrying out our days the best we could on autopilot and with no emotions. One counselor I saw regularly had developed emotions for me and my story. Damn it, this counselor, who was someone I trusted, shared his feelings for me during one of our sessions. Counseling with him was abruptly stopped.

I couldn't connect emotionally with my children. I *believed* I loved them, but I wasn't good at expressing or showing it. Emotional avoidance was what was happening. I was afraid of hugging them, of giving them any idea there was something other than love for them. For me, physical touch means something sexual – as it did with anyone who touched me. For example, with my third son, breastfeeding was the recommended way to feed him. It was gaining in popularity with pediatricians as more valuable than formula for growth and creating a bond between mother and child. Pair Bonding was recognized as vital to infants who were diagnosed with Failure to Thrive, as one of my children was. Regardless of the counseling and awareness of my lack of ability to bond, my heart ached to connect on any level with them.

I tried but I could not allow myself to relax enough to let milk flow. The thought of a baby attached to my breast was repulsive to me. Each attempt left me nauseated, triggering me repeatedly until I had to give it up in favor of our sanity and bottle feeding. This is the first time I have shared that memory. Breast-feeding is natural; however, to a sexual trauma survivor, bearing children is traumatic, and breast-feeding is traumatic. We are only learning about and sharing this tragic phenomenon today.

There was no play with my children after the birth of my second son. I tried to play some with the kids, especially if we were at the beach. I attempted to play games, coloring, and a few other kids' activities; however, I was so consumed with making sure the house was right, the job was right, that everything was in its place so my husband wasn't upset for any reason, that I didn't have any more to give to the lives I had brought into the world.

Though my awareness of good intentions was developing, through counseling and my friends, I wasn't addressing the issue of learned behaviors in myself or my children. We worked harder at hiding the truth of our past than we did in living for the present moment. We had all but forgotten about love.

Not having heard from David, my next long-term spiral into darkness began. I always did look for love in the wrong places.

*Write about how you survived with the options you knew of at the time. Offer yourself grace.*

*"Shame prevents us from receiving or giving love."*
*~ Sher Unbound*

# Eight

## The Narcissist

*"If there is one piece of wisdom you gain from me,
it's always, always, listen to your intuition."*
*~ Sher Unbound*

From the night we met, I knew it wasn't a good thing. He was too persistent, too charming, and too attentive. In the first half-hour, he seemed nice enough, and damn it – why didn't I listen to those sirens going off in the back of mind? *"Run, Run, Run!"*

I met him through my neighbors in the apartment above me. I was in the end stages of my divorce from my husband and had met David before this man. I told David about him and we talked at length about his characteristics. While David wasn't against my seeing this new guy, he had cautioned me once about his concerns surrounding his "strong" behavior.

An incident that has stayed with me occurred while I was at a gathering one night. David, the kids, and I were visiting our mutual friends, cooking out and having a pleasant evening, when we heard the engine of a motorcycle revving hard. Several of us went to the window to look for the source, and sure enough, it was him. He had followed me there. What was he thinking? I excused myself and went downstairs to ask what he thought he was doing. He threw some accusations at me in anger (attempting to make me feel cheap) as I watched him with part dismay, a little curiosity, and some irritation. He explained he was upset to find me with my friends and not him. With not much of any excuse to offer other than they were my friends, I felt compelled to reply that I would see or call him later and went back to the party. David warned me that night he'd seen behavior like this before from men, and to be careful.

I don't know why the Red Flag didn't pop up in front of me then, especially when several told me that it was out of line for him to even think of doing that – following me and making a scene. I was accustomed to seeing myself as less than worthy of respect by men, so I over-explained myself. As I write this, I am seeing more patterns of low self-worth and dysfunctional thinking.

***How many red flags does it take to get your attention?***

*"Red flags are easy to miss when boundaries are not in place."*
~ *Sher Unbound*

The kids were all about the attention he gave them. They were all about *any* attention they received. Not receiving the love from me I wanted to give them, they latched onto any attention they were given. We all did; we were the perfect set-up for what came next.

He poured his attention on them when he was around. He was into sports – that was something we were never really concerned about as a family unit before. His sports made him like a superhero to the kids. He bragged about his football days, his motorcycle, his fast car. The All-American Man. *This is important for me to note now, as it was a red flag of sorts (later) – that I had abandoned myself for the sake of making others happy.*

He had my kids hooked. My oldest even wished openly he was his dad. At first, I blew that statement off; then I saw how they each responded to him and his way of connecting to them. He was doing something that eluded me – he was connecting with them.

He voiced his temper, and the manipulation tactics increased after I was finally direct and said I wanted to break it off. I leaned into his manipulation of "all or nothing," forcing myself to believe his statement that the kids needed him. I knew I wasn't strong enough to handle his pressure at that point. The kids and I had walked that lane before. Surrendering under pressure to him, I abandoned myself once more.

I never did want this relationship. I was happy with my life as it was – dating, going out with friends, hanging out with the kids as much as I allowed myself to (trying to connect), and generally living. Dating him was fun, so long as I followed "his" rules and wants. I would have appreciated him more as a friend, not anything more.

We began dating regularly, and honestly, I have a hard time remembering the exact timeline of how things happened because I was detached emotionally, on multiple anti-psychotic pills, drinking more than was necessary, and depressed.

David had stopped writing completely – it was almost like he never existed. There were a few times this man read notes to me from David and was openly jealous of him, accusing me of sleeping with him. That was a glaring Red Flag that I picked up on and chose to ignore. I was looking out for the long-term picture of life and my plan wasn't looking so good. I was working a lot and this guy was willing to help me with the kids. He was inserting himself into every corner of my life while I held the door open.

Before long, we were leaving my beloved California, believing there would be a better life elsewhere. While not the worst mistake I made in my life, it was not one of my better decisions. Self-abandonment had been completed.

*Have you ever become so detached you lost yourself?*

*"Home isn't always where the heart is."*
*~ Sher Unbound*

# Nine

## Nebraska

*"When I am asked how I came here, I often reply,*
*'I was stranded here.'"*
*~ Sher Unbound*

Telling people, "I was stranded here" is not quite truthful. It was a way to accept and resolve that in my mind it was my choice to come here. This was my pattern: to run away, always hoping to find a way to escape my past. Moving to Nebraska was the only option in my current frame of mind.

Okay, let me say this first. It does have charm. It's safe, has beautiful winters and short summers. The sandhills and rivers possess their own stunning views and beauty. Every place I've ever lived I've been able to find positives in.

The most difficult was the culture shock for each of the kids and me. We went from living the free West Coast lifestyle to the Midwest, where it was almost too laid back. My California-style clothing was traded for jeans, oversized shirts, and hoodies. Not all of Nebraska is this way – this is me trying to fit into the background, unobserved like thousands of others.

*Write about a place your heart is called to.*

*"You just make do with what you have and give it the best you got."*
~ *Sher Unbound*

It was slowly happening all over again, but then again, with an awareness of what was happening after my last psychiatric hospital stay. History was repeating itself, *had* repeated itself. Let me clarify that – I was seeing the same patterns develop in my significant other as I had seen in my first husband and in myself, only better hidden in psychological abuse. Gaslighting was the worst I ever experienced in my life. That drove me to believe the multiple diagnoses I'd been given of emotional instability. The doctors were more than happy to prescribe me multiple medications, which my significant other happily approved of.

*This is the perfect place to speak about this point in time. Living over-medicated and day drinking to numb any feeling that was not already buried was my norm. There is so much of this relationship that feels missing – conversations between him and me are almost blotted out. Living out of body, or so it seemed, was the only way to cope with how little I thought of myself and my life. It is, without a doubt, more painful than the sexual abuse as a child. Trying to find what I felt about my experiences in these years is still something I am challenged with today.*

The most noticeable pattern was his temper and his jealousy. The effects of his jealousy were expressed through constant verbal barbs about David, never satisfied with any answer that was given. It was peculiar to me he could be jealous of someone that was a best friend to me and the kids. He checked the mileage on the car to make sure I wasn't going any place other than I was supposed to. His temper would flare if he lost at anything, and he wasn't doing well with holding civilian jobs. I saw the red flags but felt defeated with my depression and anxiety, sinking deeper into myself every day.

Isolated far away from anything remotely like home, I tried to make friends and find work, overworking in the house, trying to make it a decent place to live. I tried to fit in, telling myself I liked the country music, the way of life, and the laid-back environment. It was probably mid-way through our life in a small town in the northern part of the state that my emotional breakdown began. I have never been more appreciative of how the mind works than in that time.

My breakdown showed me who I wasn't, and what I needed to do.

*Write about a time or times you leaned into and trusted intuition.*

*"If you ever loved me, you'll let me go."*
*~ Sher Unbound*

I stayed out of body as much as possible and resisted connecting with anyone. My weight ballooned to 300 pounds. My movements were robotic, rote in nature, and I gave up on looking for common factors to relate to this man who was slowly twisting my brain into something unrecognizable. The only common factor was our last name and shared address.

My attempts to ignore him moved to encouraging him to find activities other than me. Several times I tried to convince him we weren't compatible and to let me go. These efforts were met with manipulation that wore me down, draining me of any of the energy that I had gathered to bring up the topic.

Though I loved my children dearly, I still had no connection to them on an emotional level. My efforts at bonding failed with all four children. Each child was hurting physically, emotionally, and spiritually and their treatment from the narcissist was not helping matters. The guilt I felt of my inability to show love weighed on me with oppression, forming into a deep depression; I felt helpless as my sweet children lashed out at themselves and me.

The secrets and lies held inside over the years began to take their toll on me. Keeping the truth from myself, lying by omission over the years, masked me, my life, and who I was. Looking in the mirror at a woman who physically was me, but not recognizing her, was the equivalent of a mini-existential crisis. My appearance grew drab, plain, like someone who didn't care. It was hard to see myself in a window reflection, picture, or mirror. If I could give any description of a monster it would have my name on it.

Being miserable and challenged by PTSD and agoraphobia led to too much alcohol, pain killers for phantom pains, and anti-anxiety pills. At other times I was totally dry of everything. Those were the worst because I was still showing the symptoms of being on everything. They call it "dry drunk." I sought healing in about every way available: therapy, PT, psychiatric treatment, pills, potions, elixirs, sex, and religion; nothing worked. I attempted suicide once by trying to drive the car into a light pole, swerving off the road before the car made an impact. There was a landslide happening and it was gaining momentum, taking me with it.

*How do we ask for help when we don't know what we need?*

*"You can dig your grave when you have
been on the ground long enough
there's no place else to go."*
~ Sher Unbound

# Ten

## The Sparrow

*"How do we help the lost when we don't even know
who we are?"*
*~ Sher Unbound*

The tears started in the morning. By mid-afternoon, not having moved from the chair, heavy sobs continued with painful contractions of my ribs and stomach.

A pause for a few moments to rest, breathe, and begin again. My memories don't include what started the tears other than surrender; there was no energy left to fight, nothing left to fight for. My soul was someplace else, not in me.

"Call Pastor," I said to my son when he asked if he could help me.

My daughter sat on the floor next to me, quietly playing with her dolls. A mirror facing me reflected someone that I didn't recognize. I noticed the room – my sewing machine, the desk, the chair underneath me, my daughter, my son. The reflection of myself in the mirror. The thoughts were an attempt to ground myself, to gain some form of reality.

My pastor arrived at the house and sat with me, speaking in low, soft tones while on several calls; then she asked me questions: "Do you know where you are? Do you know the date? Do you want to pray?"

Sometime that same day she asked me to go with her. I put on my shoes and she gently asked me, "Are you ready?" I blindly nodded yes, with no idea of what there was to be ready for.

We drove quietly, music playing on the radio. Every now and then she'd ask if I wanted to stop for anything. No.

Rain began to fall that morning, continuing through the day. The rhythm of the rain seemed to match my tears. My words were interrupted with tears when there was a need to speak. Checked in, a building full of people, psych techs, nurses, and doctors. I never felt more alone in my life than in that moment.

Alone in a room, wrapped in a blanket, legs curled under me on a window seat. I made a mental note it was still raining. How long had it rained today? Was the earth crying too? It had been raining so long it was as if the universe was crying with me.

Numb. No feelings, no cares. I began to speak out loud to no one – maybe the universe, maybe God. More grounding: a window, a bed, a chair, a door that must be the bathroom. A closet. No pictures but plenty of cameras. Body check: my chest hurt. My eyes felt like they were open in a sandstorm, stinging and swollen. My hands were clenched. My jaw hurt for some reason. "Just make it stop. Let me sleep." My voice had returned.

More silence, and it was as heavy as my heart and body. I was looking through blurry eyes out the window facing me. Outside of the window was a brook with a lush green lawn surrounding it. Nothing was really registering, just objects and silence. It was still raining.

A small sparrow landed on a rock in the brook. It was still sprinkling some, then raining and back to sprinkles. The sparrow was flapping its wings like it was enjoying the soft rain. Its head raised up slightly, more flapping, a shudder of its tiny body. It was alone, like me.

Sitting on the window seat doing nothing more than observing the sparrow, I spoke out loud to it. My eyes were focused on that little bird and I began pouring my pain out. The more I talked the less I cried, and the more the sparrow seemed to listen. *I felt heard.*

I thanked the sparrow for listening to me. No, I didn't think this was odd considering I was in a psychiatric unit. I appreciated the bird sitting there listening to me. There was a feeling of something more than pain and sadness coming through – pure appreciation.

After a few moments of silence between us and watching one another, the sparrow flew up and perched on the ledge of the window outside. I didn't see its eyes but we both knew I would be all right. I whispered, "Thank you" softly once more and touched the window. When I touched it with my fingertips, a flow of warm calmness went through me – entering through my fingers, filling my body with what felt like a warm flow of water.

I could feel.

*Have you ever felt so empty that even desperation felt good because it was a feeling?*

*"Nothing is clearer than the moment you
lose your mind."*
*~ Sher Unbound*

# Eleven

# Life Part II

*"His last kiss was his last breath of life,
living in my soul for eternity."*
*~ Sher Unbound*

*"Focusing our attention only on the act separates us
from embracing the entire point of the play."*
~ Sher Unbound

Exploring my role in that past relationship uncovered the gift of compassion, love, and understanding for myself and this personality. The lessons I took away were not obvious to me when I ended the relationship because of the depletion of love's energy. People are placed in our paths for a reason, sometimes to show us what we need to do to achieve the highest versions of ourselves.

*During my years of college, my children experienced many challenges. We were fractured as a family, and that was a constant worry on my mind while trying to attend classes, study, work, and try and have some form of social life. While I would love to expand on my children, for their privacy, I won't be adding their story to the remainder of this journal.*

Knowing I needed to do something with my life, it was time to explore my opportunities for my future. Under consideration was teaching or reaching out to others who had been challenged with life situations like mine. I decided to enroll as a non-traditional student in State College and proudly graduated six years later with a B.S. in Social Work and Counseling – with Honors.

I had *no business* thinking of entertaining anyone, and the men who were attracted to me were less than what ought to have been on my radar. After a year or so of bad luck with dating, I decided not to date, placing my focus on my children and their needs while working a few different jobs in my chosen field of social work after graduation.

**What do you take with you into any new relationship?**

*"Love the person, not the idea of them."*
~ *Sher Unbound*

One afternoon while on the clock for a local shelter, I saw him. This tall, handsome man, who appeared to be single. Sherri, I told myself, you have no business dating, no business thinking of dating; but he was *"F - I - N – E."* Tall, very tall, handsome, and he moved with a peaceful walk that simply said, "I'm chill."

Making excuses and volunteer trips back to the shelter where I saw him last in his yard next door became a mission. Every day, just after 4:00 PM he would be home, watering the lawn, sipping on a cold beer, or mowing. I'm certain he saw me and was just playing it cool.

One of those days I would drive by or make excuses to sneak looks at him. I missed him. He wasn't home and I felt a little sadness inside. I shrugged it off; it was time to drive home to my apartment and begin my usual routine of dropping the purse on the stairs, kicking off my shoes, flipping on the computer, and grabbing some tea. I lived alone now, and my computer and books kept me company. The one thing I enjoyed the most was that I was *free*.

I was catching up on the news and chatting with my son online. Someone was complaining about women in the chat room we were in and he wasn't happy in the least. I dropped the message that if he needed to talk, he was more than welcome to message me. I didn't expect him to respond but he did, privately.

When he turned on his camera I was stunned. It was *him*. In my chat and on video. The man from the yard next door to the shelter. Wait, what? *Him?* I had to talk to him but didn't turn on my camera. Something told me to wait. We chatted a few minutes and signed off and he was calmer after we spoke.

I had to do my usual drive by the shelter the next day. When I pulled into the parking lot of the shelter, he wasn't there. No! What was this? Maybe he changed his work hours? It happens. Okay. Leave it be. Go home and do the usual. Forget it, Sher. You aren't interested in dating, remember?

*How do you quiet your intuition?*

*"I just want to see you again."*
~ *Sher Unbound*

We chatted online again and this time he asked me for my number. He learned where I lived in town and we made arrangements to talk on the phone. We chatted about coffee, the cool new coffee shop in town, our likes, birthdays, and the fact that his birthday was the day we met online.

I had a busy workweek that week, but was only too happy to make time to speak to him, except we never got to that next call before I landed in the hospital with my back out from pinched nerves. Some life events stay with you forever, like injuries received from domestic violence.

He phoned me on my cell while in the hospital, and after explaining why I could not meet him for coffee, he said, "Say no more. I'll bring it to you."

I woke at one point to see a delicious bag of divine aromatic coffee and a cookie to go with it. He attached a note that read, "Looking forward to our date."

A date! He was asking me out on a genuine date! I absolutely had to get home now.

Living in a basement apartment was a bit of a challenge because of the long flight of stairs, but I made it work. We talked on the phone and finally arranged our first date, where the first kiss happened under the most brilliant summer night sky. This is one of the bittersweet memories, as it was on my birthday. He took me to dinner, talked, and laughed quite a lot. There was a moment where I laughed at myself when he said, "Please tell me you aren't one of those women who is afraid to eat? I love this place and I'm hungry." After a hearty meal, we decided to walk it off at the park located just two blocks from where we later bought our home. I'll leave that there.

Over the next few years, we traveled, went on weekend gigs, crossed the country on road trips, went to concerts, and frequently enjoyed camping, canoeing, walking, movies, and books. It sounds perfect, right? We were the best of friends, accepting our differences, even working around a few; however, there were some we could never work through and we made the mistake of ignoring the elephant in the room.

*What are some of your most memorable moments with your best friend?*

*"Sometimes it's the memories we miss,*
*not the person."*
~ *Sher Unbound*

I knew going into the marriage that it probably wasn't the best bet for us. We both were settling for one another out of loneliness and not wanting to grow old alone. Neither of us had a secure attachment style, but we worked around it and made it work for us.

An hour before the wedding was to start, I hadn't gotten dressed yet. Was this the right thing to do? Why was I marrying him? Why were we getting married? Was it for love? Did we need to make it official to maintain what we held between us? *There's the avoidance.*

I made it on time to the wedding site with a few moments to spare. The officiant was a few minutes late, so I had time to compose myself and say hello to the guests before we said "I do." I didn't feel any different, and we both were exhausted when we left for our week-long honeymoon. Disaster upon disaster began during the week ahead of the wedding date and continued throughout the honeymoon. Most we laughed off, but living with more awareness now, I wonder how many signs there were not to marry.

Finding solid proof *(meeting her)* of his infidelity, once before the marriage and then after, was hard to take. Living with the knowledge was worse. There were a lot of red flags signaling this behavior before we married, but to keep him in my life I turned my head with a pain that felt like being gut-punched.

We got on well enough, but his habits hurt – a lot. I was willing to exchange that part of us to not lose his companionship and friendship.

*Have you ever dated or entered a new relationship out of loneliness? What is your attachment style?*

*"The hardest thing you will ever do is face yourself."*
*~ Sher Unbound*

Old habits die hard. I had a strong resistance then to facing the truth about my feelings, and it was showing up in how I allowed some of his habits to invade our marital space, such as other women, bouts of heavier drinking, and never finishing what he started. There was a lot of procrastination, where he'd get something going and never get the job done.

We took good care of one another physically, held good conversations, and were compatible in almost every way, except both of us were emotionally unavailable and co-dependent. We were over-polite to each other to compensate for our individual growing emotional needs, needs we were not aware of.

We did have common interests, and we tried to travel as much as we could, sharing passions in history, the arts, music, and many more things. Camping was a favorite pastime of ours, as was gardening. He knew I was relentless in my work, no matter what career I chose – Business Woman or Executive Director. He supported my ambitions and I reciprocated with support for his interests and ambitions when he expressed them.

What an odd couple we were, both needy in all realms of life, and yet secretly supportive of each other's unhealthy ways.

*What do you sacrifice for the sake of being in a relationship?*

*"It worked until it didn't."*
*~ Sher Unbound*

Less than ten years into our marriage, our lives were turned upside down. We had been working on inner work – each of us. Getting healthier, feeling good about who we were as a couple, talking about the emotional unavailability, supporting each other in our efforts to have the marriage work "till death do we part."

We bought a home just up the street from where we shared our first kiss. A few short years after we moved into our new home, 2017 pitched us a curveball that was a sure swing and a hit, knocking us into orbit.

Depression was taking over our home because of illness, death, and the placement of one of our grandchildren with us. I was putting on a lot of weight from stress eating and I was swamped with work, which created large amounts of stress on me. My husband began increasingly missing days of work in the winter of 2017. This continued until January of 2018, when he saw our doctor only after his employer insisted he go or risk suspension for lack of performance.

He was diagnosed with cancer in February of 2018; in March we said goodbye to our beloved pet; then in May of that same year, my father died.

I kissed my husband the final time on June 22, 2018, holding his last breath inside me forever.

***What has been your experience with depression and death?***

*"We weren't finished yet, M'love."*
*~ Sher Unbound*

It felt like my breath had been sucked out of me with that last kiss. The world started to spin. The sun was too bright. It was cold. I was hot. I was confused. And in some sort of hyper-awareness mode, not listening to anyone, all I could think was, "Where is he?" And I was angry, hurt, and frightened. I felt abandoned. More alone than ever before with so many people around.

People were talking too loudly. *Too loud... too loud! Shut the fuck up, everyone! Go away! Let me think!* were my only thoughts in that moment. I hadn't smoked in seven years and remember feeling like I was going to pass out after the first puff.

I tossed the cigarette down in the yard, then wandered around some. A policeman came and asked me to go sit down. The woman from Hospice was there and kept telling me about the process of grieving, asking me if there was anything she could do. Are you serious? Go away. Just go away. All I want is to be alone. With my thoughts. Our thoughts. His last breath. Give me mine...

***Have you ever discovered what love is after it's gone? Even unhealthy love?***

*"You didn't fight! Damn it, why didn't you fight?"*
*~ Sher Unbound*

# Twelve

## *Intent*

*"It's not that I can't, I don't want to. I'm done."*
*~ Sher Unbound*

I couldn't bear the firsts. I'm strong, but those were hard anniversary dates to see come and I was grateful at the end of each day to see them pass.

Only a few weeks before he passed, we spent our ten-year anniversary in his hospital room sharing his waking hours. He had the nurses bring in lunch and roses for me that day. My heart was swept away with the knowledge he was trying, even when in pain, to share his feelings.

My first birthday without him, first Christmas, first New Year. His death anniversary, our wedding anniversary, and his birthday. The death of our pet. The passing of my father was hard to bear as well – for obvious conflicting emotional reasons.

I had to raise my grandson alone now. That came with additional responsibilities and legal matters to attend to, reporting, and his monthly welfare visits by social workers while trying to help him navigate his world of upside-down feelings of loss. There was mounting pressure from the bank about the mortgage, taking a crash course in personal finances, insurance, and learning to navigate the legal system when it comes to rights of survivorship.

There was another death I was mourning – my own. When he passed, my identity went with him. All that I knew of who I was, was gone in one final kiss.

***How do you cope with trauma anniversaries?***

*"All that I knew of who I was, was gone in
one final kiss."*
~ *Sher Unbound*

Now it's time to dismantle a life no longer present. The task of taking apart and putting away or giving away what a person leaves behind is much like attending the funeral all over again if there's not enough time to process the loss. This was our life, his life. He kept everything. He finished nothing but kept everything.

There was so much to clean out, and with each item, I said more goodbyes, growing more depressed. Was this all there was after all those years together? I wanted *him* back, not the accumulated meaningless piles of nothing.

Many days I resisted the urge to put a giant "For Sale" sign on everything and just leave, to go anywhere but here. Through all this, there was the undeniable fact a young boy needed me to hold myself together. There were more needs to address, such as income – how would I make up for the loss of my husband's income? I had to increase my business revenue. More hours working, less time living. That was fine for me because it also meant less time caring for myself.

People tend to think that after a few months or a year you pick up your life and get on with it again after a spouse has died. Nothing could be further from the truth. Who you are dies with them.

You lose the person you were and for an anxious, guilt-ridden, co-dependent to have their world suddenly stop existing... I was in a full existential crisis. Everything about me had changed in a matter of a few short moments, and those changes weren't being recognized. There was only the drive to go through the motions and keep going because deep inside my resiliency was telling me to keep going for my grandson, not for me.

Your name stays the same, but nothing else about you does. Sleep evades you, your health can go to pieces, any emotions you held are washed away with the few or many tears that you cry. You are not the one the bank wants to speak to; they want to speak to the "head of household." You are not the one the insurance company deals with, only the head of household. Who was I? Did I even matter? Was I invisible?

Routines stop, daily enjoyment of anything stops. Sex begins to seem like a faded memory. Until you force yourself to have sex with someone or yourself out of the need to feel.

My grandson and I have muddled through a lot of depression, anger, and happy moments together since death visited our home. We're finding our steps together, and I gave him this one piece of advice. I recently had to remind him of this commitment, as his own mother has been diagnosed with ovarian cancer. Breathe, Sher. Just Breathe.

*"We are like a Superhero Team. We're at odds, each of us with our special power, and though we may argue sometimes, we still have each other's backs all the time."*

**Do you give yourself care and love?**

*"I got you. We're a superhero team, remember?"*
*~ Sher Unbound*

Anger filled me one morning as my eyes opened and it struck me there was no one next to me. The tears came within minutes before my brain was engaged. It wasn't the need of anyone, or a someone; it was a need for him to be there. The other part of me! I felt nothing but anger, and it was directed at someone who only existed in memory. I missed him; it wasn't supposed to be like this. This wasn't the plan or what he promised.

We were in the middle of getting our lives together, becoming a family and learning about ourselves. He left something else unfinished for me to tie up the loose ends: our life together.

**In what ways do you work out the emotions you feel when they seem confusing?**

*"You see no choices. I see one more left."*
*~ Sher Unbound*

And then without a warning, my plan for suicide. I was beyond tired. My life had no meaning, no feelings were left, and I believed there was no purpose for my existence.

It's all there ever was – no living, just existing, much as I had done as a teen. All there was to me was an ugly, useless, fat, old woman with no future, no feelings, and nothing to offer to anyone, let alone a child. Who wanted this? I didn't. What would it hurt if I left the world? Who would care? Really?

The transition was over. I was alone and raising a child at my age. No vision for the future except what others believed I could be doing or *should* be doing with my life.

**What does hope look like to you?**

*"This wasn't the choice I had in mind."*
*~ Sher Unbound*

After a few very unsatisfying dates only for sex, it dawned on me that not one man could make me feel anything. I couldn't feel anything, so how would they be able to find something in me? There was no connection; not even a little. What was the use? I saw nothing but a fuck-up when I looked in the mirror. It was a joke that I was even trying to make any day count.

Taking my life was on my mind heavily every day. I began my plan, working out how I would leave a note for my grandson and my kids, and instructions, which I had no idea if anyone would care to follow. Most would be pissed that I left a child so selfishly.

The night finally arrived, and my grandson was sleeping. Lying down, my favorite station turned on low with my pills next to me, it hit me. This was it. Final. I had doubts that were focused on what if it failed? What if all I got was sick to my stomach? Fucking doubts – that's all there had been for months. I doubted everything.

I slammed my fists down on the bed next to my sides, kicking my legs in anger, wanting to scream, and couldn't do it; it would wake up my grandson. *Nothing worked.* I tried to scream into the pillow, cry, hit something. Nothing would come out. This too? Was there anything that I couldn't fuck up? Oh, good lord, I couldn't even cry? What the fuck ever; go figure.

*Nothing is ever worth taking your life for. Not a person, not an emotion. NOTHING. If you ever get to this point – reach out to someone. ANYONE. Talk, scream, run, walk... whatever it takes.*

*"Fucking doubts – that's all there had been for months.*
*I doubted everything."*
*~ Sher Unbound*

Numb, no tears, only mounting anger at myself for my situation. I ran through all the ways I was fucking this up and in frustration grabbed my phone. I had hoped to find something on suicide or someone to talk to.

Scrolling my apps, absent of feeling, a post signature line caught my attention and I paused to read it. A young man, looking quite pleased with himself in his image, caught my attention. It was his tagline that made me pay attention.

I read the post and it made no sense to me. Who the hell writes this stuff? I wondered. The signature line was "Fear Less. Love More." I rolled it over again in my mind. Fear Less. Love More. *What the fuck did that mean?*

I read it repeatedly. *One click* and I found an online group that was different. The posts were all of hope, good feelings, and happy people, so I continued scrolling, reading more with some jealousy and awe.

I forgot about taking the pills and kept reading with a sense of wonder, looking into who this person was that wrote the tag line. Then I went back to the post I found it. Huh. He's a kid, I thought. What does he know? When I tossed the phone aside, it was almost morning and I had forgotten about the pills but learned something important.

There was an ounce of hope there might be a chance.

*Have you ever experienced a change that was profound, but you were unaware of it?*

*"I held an ounce of hope that I might have a chance.*
*I just might."*
*~ Sher Unbound*

How were these people all so positive, so happy? Didn't they have trauma and drama? Post after post of ascension, love, light, be positive, we're all happy and, ah, there it is... there *was* sadness in the past, but they found a way to rise above it.

They were talking of ascent – of rising above the mess their lives were before. They wrote of high self-esteem, of healing inner wounds, of love. *I wanted that!* How did I get what they have?

Meh, not me. They are all probably born *good people* – not like me. Dirty, ruined, over-sexed, old, and incapable of love. I wouldn't even let people hug me or shake my hand, let alone try and pretend I'm good enough for this wonderful thing they all shared.

What the heck, I thought. There's nothing to lose, and I clicked the request to join. Uh... that was a surprise! They accepted me! It was like getting a new credit card with unlimited use! I kept going back to the page. The more I read and interacted, the better it felt. I found someplace that fit and that I could relate to. Gradually, I was accepted as part of the group of regulars.

*Do you think you have standards to meet before you are "good enough?"*

*"Being accepted is only part of the process.*
*Accepting yourself is the rest."*
*~Sher Unbound*

Was there a good person inside of me? Was I not made to be a sex toy or someone's punching bag? Was there a light inside of me that could be a beacon of hope in the same way others were?

The thought of wanting to die was fading, being replaced with a desire to find ways to live a little better, a little happier, with more care and concern for how I treated myself. Each day I climbed a little higher. There were days of depression mixed in, but more good days than not. I stopped dating altogether and began to work through the grieving process.

Something inside me was different. It felt good to wake up. I saw something *good* inside. *I was starting to like myself.*

**What do you want to offer yourself at this moment?**

*"It takes compassion and understanding
to appreciate what we see inside us."*
~ *Sher Unbound*

Maybe the right questions or going through my timeline will show me specific points of my rise – like the Lotus that pushes through the murky, muddy waters to unfold and stand tall in the sunlight each morning. It started slow but then after a few weeks, the shedding of layer after layer of old patterns began, and as each layer fell away, I felt better.

I knew this change would take time and work, but I was choosing this change. I decided to take back my life, my power. There would be the moment of meeting my false self and telling her it was time to leave. My mind was set to start living with purpose.

There is a story that came to me one morning as I was taking an inventory of my life, my journey, and how fast my life was becoming unbound. This is that story.

*Own Your Worth*

*Evening would come soon. Sun was feeling more relaxed, exerting less energy as is customary this time of day. Moon began barely showing a hint of soft white light. Activity in the Great Pond, slow and melodic, the way an orchestra begins to warm up before a grand opus. D'Anne Da'Lion, off in the short grasses, had been particularly observant and grew agitated throughout the day.*

*Watching from a distance, D'Anne Da'Lion allowed feelings of doubt to flow through the bright yellow petals all day. No one mentioned it, no one asked what was causing the low vibration. "Typical. I am insignificant," D'Anne Da'Lion noted at one point. "Humans come and sit to admire Lotus Love, filled with the desire to own it for themselves. They admire and fawn over Iris and all the other great creatures of the Pond," D'Anne thought while sulking.*

*D'Anne Da'Lion broke into the activity of preparing for Moon to lead the orchestration of the evening opus by abruptly asking, "Why do I choose to Survive? What is so special about Lotus Love and all the others? I am worthy of more!"*

*Pause. All preparation stopped suddenly, leaving an opening for D'Anne Da'Lion to continue. Lotus Love thought, "Incredible! D'Anne is ready!"*

*Historically, the family of D'Anne Da'Lion would only submit to the routine of life and death without once claiming their value. They are without question one of the most significant of the Great Pond's flora.*

*"An affirmation of Worth! Incredible!" Lotus Love proclaimed to all in the Great Pond. For dramatic impact, Lotus Love paused a moment more before answering. Deliberately choosing the response, Lotus replied, "I've seen you in a lower vibration today but made the choice to ignore it. You needed to be able to ask that question for yourself. It is time you acknowledge and own your worth."*

*D'Anne Da'Lion quipped back rapidly, "Needed to ask? Why did I need to ask? Why am I ignored? You are seen all day. Humans come all day to observe you, paint your portrait. Pray over you and bless you. All desire to own you. Iris stands tall above the others, dancing with Wind when it comes to the Great Pond. Lovers come to absorb your essence, Lotus Love. Every creature in the Great Pond pleases so many and serves those who visit us. I am stepped on, plucked, and cursed. Look how Reed makes a special barrier for you. Iris has a community of their own. I am here, away from most of you, alone to fend for myself and abused. Did you know my family has been nearly wiped out from the Human dwellings?"*

*Again, deliberately choosing the right words, Lotus Love spoke. "You needed to ask because you have ignored your value. You allowed your doubt to lead you to the Awareness of your worth. Now it is time for you to openly acknowledge your own Love. You are of great importance and significance in the plan of the Great Pond."*

*D'Anne Da'Lion was beginning to fold the soft petals inward, feeling unheard. Lotus Love spoke softly, "D'Anne. it is not with harshness or lack of care I speak to you in this way. It is time for you to recognize, appreciate, and own your value. You don't want to be treated in this way any longer, correct?"*

*"No, I do not. I am worthy of Love and respect," D'Anne Da'Lion replied adamantly.*

*"Then state your value," Lotus Love said with finality.*

*D'Anne Da'Lion paused and thought a moment. Pausing in folding the soft yellow petals, she began to speak.*

*"I am NOT common. I AM unique. I CAN give hope and bring magic to those who place their wishes with me to carry them to the Great Universe. I AM Persistent. I AM Magic, I AM Choice, I AM Free, I AM determined, I AM Playful, I AM Wise, I AM Discernment, I AM Willing, I AM Trust, I AM Adventure, I AM Creator, I AM Happy, I AM Present, I AM Intent, I AM Deliberate, I AM Energy, I AM Sensible, I AM Singular, I AM Love. I AM More."*

*All who could hear were quiet. Moon was beaming and dropped its soft full light directly on D'Anne Da'Lion. Lotus Love spoke. "You did not say you are a Survivor. That is because you know you are More than a Survivor. You ARE all you said and so much More. You can transform. You are a creator. You transform life through hope. You are medicine for those who know this magic. You flourish, and each time you are cut down you come back stronger. You have one root, that is strong, and you bloom into a flower of which every part of you is Love. You sustain your future with the ability to share all this without thought. Love is the More."*

*Lotus Love paused and quietly spoke. "Do you know what our source of life is? Self-Validation. The Great Pond relies on Self-Love and the Self-Validation that we ARE all you spoke of for yourself and More. If that Love vanishes, we perish. Therefore, we ignored you today. We see the Moreness and know it is something we cannot possess because it is YOURS to own and accept. Do you believe what you spoke of your Being?"*

*"I do," said D'Anne Da'Lion. "I AM Significant." D'Anne Da'Lion looked out across the field toward all in the Great Pond with Love and appreciation one final time before folding in and preparing the magic that was D'Anne's alone to own. "I am More than Significant. I AM Love."*

**Set your intent.**

*"How do I release all this rage? The pain inside?"*
*I asked her. "Set your intent."*
*What the F... I thought. Set my intent.*
*For what? I just want to feel again.*
*~ Sher Unbound*

# Epilogue

My entire life I hated myself and everything about me. It was hard work liking myself, but "love" myself? No, I believed I wasn't capable.

*And there she was.*

In the mirror one evening. She took a picture of herself and her reflection. Smiling. There were tears before the picture was taken and tears after, but she liked who she was, and how fucking strong and courageous! The beauty in her image was the courage that was powering through in that one moment. She was loving who she saw.

It was hard to see herself in her own eyes, but at the same time empowering. The feeling after seeing the image inspired her to be More. Not More as in famous or a following, but More for herself. She wanted to be the best woman she could be for herself.

That night was her turning point toward love. Finding intimate, deep, profoundly moving love. She didn't have to search far. It was in her all along.

There had been days of internal searching, releasing memories with tears and laughter while keeping what mattered – her soul intact. Letting go. Sharing her story with good intent. Sharing her life with others so they can heal and have hope in this life. Sharing her love. Watching her grow.

I was loving her and what I was seeing.

The other day, after a long talk with a deeply beautiful person, I fell in love. Not with the person I was speaking to, but with myself. *With Sher.* I never experienced love in this manner. Open, no expectations, no promises, nothing to lose. Just knowing her courage, the light inside her, and the goodness she possesses made me love her. She let go and let love. She had begun the process of shedding the baggage that was too heavy. She was starting new and was eager to learn.

I love myself. I won't even try to describe what that's like. I only wish you to know it for yourself – to know what loving yourself really means. To know peace when you sleep, the euphoric beats of music as you dance, the notes of love when you sing. To taste food for the first time without guilt. To dream and know you can make those dreams happen. To wish and know you can achieve those wishes. To just exist without internal emotional pain or guilt. To believe you have the authority to love and live fully, with wonder and excitement, and want to share that with everyone. To love your past and appreciate the gifts given. I want that for you as much as I have it within.

I will be following up with a book on the journey and the processes I took to get to this point. It is my hope each of you reading will be able to reach the level of forgiveness and understanding I have.

*"Forgiveness is Understanding."* When we can grasp the concept of what story our abusers were living when they made the choice to hurt us, the process of forgiveness comes a little easier.

My father was rejected by the women in his life he was closest to. While it does not excuse his actions toward me, understanding he was coming from the pain of rejection helped me to see his humanity and not paint him as a monster.

My ex was forced into a marriage neither of us wanted to be in.

My biological mother came from a family of fractured stories and most likely not much was shared in the way of feelings. My narcissist had his own story of pain and my late husband a deeper pain of rejection and fear of abandonment. Everyone I came across had a story – we all do.

So much of what I lived through depended on several things I was missing in my life: love, trust, acceptance, boundaries, and values. There was one other gift to me that needed to be opened: the gift of choice. All along there was the ability to choose my path, and until I embraced that concept, there was never going to be change.

Without having learned any of these, I was destined to react, not respond. I was bound to not understand and always live in fear. When the basics of humanity are not laid as the foundation, any life we try to build will not stand.

Write. Discover. Feel. I hope your journaling brings to light some of the deeper meaning behind the trauma you faced. If not deeper meaning, a hope for clarity and/or closure.

# 100 Days of Intent

Setting an intent is you making a commitment to yourself. It's you saying you have something to achieve or something in your life you want. It's committing to fulfill your needs in any area of your life.

An intention ought to tie closely to your inner thoughts, values, and life view. They can be clear and concise or a simple concept you want to become aligned with. Try to keep your intentions positive; if you say you want to be less afraid, try writing and saying, "I want to be vulnerable and courageous." See the difference?

When you set your intent, use the following as a guide. Then, using this page or a journal, write your specific intentions in the space below.

- During meditation time is the best place to plant the seeds of your intent. Try to perform your meditations first thing in the morning (schedule permitting).
- Your higher self knows if your intent is coming from want or need. It will be best planted when you are in a state of deeper contentment and reflection.
- Detach from the outcome. It does not matter the result; the focus is stating your need.
- Let go of the details. Do not try to control your intent once you have stated it.

- An intention is not a goal. It's the outcome of that goal. The difference is between "going to do" and "are" doing. State it as if it is happening now.
  - o  Goal – I will say I'm sorry to my family and friends for the wrongs I have made.
  - o  Intent – I am creating and sharing an environment of peace.
- Check back in frequently with your intent. How is the progress? Write or record what you are experiencing.

Ask yourself these questions to get you started on writing your intentions.

- What is important to you?
- Is there something you want to let go of or let pass through?
- Is there a dream you must create something?
- What does your higher self look like?
- Are you holding resentments in your life?
- What does your highest self feel like?
- What are you most proud of?
- What word(s) would you like to align yourself with?
- What do you want to release in fears, anger, resentment?
- What do you appreciate or feel grateful for?

# 100 Days of Intentions.

I want/need to...

1. practice speaking in a kind tone of voice.
2. be vulnerable in sharing my feelings.
3. share my ideas openly.
4. journal every day.
5. leave my house at least once a day.
6. walk more.
7. be aware of being aware.
8. be earnest.
9. hear more.
10. sleep better.
11. understand others more.
12. practice compassion.
13. forgive easily.
14. release grudges.
15. practice appreciation.
16. express gratitude.
17. be certain.
18. be more proactive, less reactive.
19. practice power pauses.
20. think things through to the end.
21. trust myself.
22. hear me.
23. hold space for myself and others.

24. open my mind daily.
25. meditate.
26. improve my nutrition.
27. honor my body.
28. feed my mind.
29. practice positivity.
30. release regrets.
31. say I love you.
32. reduce my bubble.
33. shift my perspective.
34. stretch throughout the day.
35. relax each day.
36. speak to one new person each day.
37. return calls via phone, not texts.
38. practice patience.
39. be discerning.
40. say no when I want to say no.
41. accept my shortcomings.
42. improve my vocabulary.
43. prioritize.
44. be more connected.
45. be more decisive.
46. choose my words carefully.
47. be at peace.
48. worry less.
49. think positively.
50. speak positively.
51. act according to what's appropriate for me.
52. be impeccable.
53. finish what I start.
54. embrace discomfort when I need to.
55. set my mood each morning.

56. set my intent each day.
57. be more.
58. be strategic.
59. love more.
60. fear less.
61. be humble.
62. self-check every day for mood and intent.
63. place myself first.
64. leverage concepts to my benefit.
65. say it in my own words.
66. be more hyper selective.
67. maintain persistence.
68. be determined.
69. let feelings flow through me.
70. maintain independence.
71. develop power habits.
72. break old habits.
73. remain fluid.
74. love unconditionally.
75. embrace love toward myself.
76. invite others into my circle.
77. enjoy goodness in others.
78. have fewer expectations.
79. say what I mean.
80. take things less personally.
81. allow intimacy into my life.
82. work through triggers.
83. search for my own solutions.
84. seek help when I need to.
85. ask questions.
86. suspend judgments.
87. freely forgive myself and others.

88. accept change as it comes.
89. have less resistance to change.
90. maintain my finances.
91. utilize the tools available for self-care.
92. create an aesthetic environment.
93. keep my environment peaceful.
94. just be.
95. be aware of my purpose.
96. be aware of changes in my being always.
97. take time to play.
98. live a balanced life.
99. feel love and acceptance from my relationships.
100. live a life of service to others that best suits my purpose in life.

# Author Bio

Unbind, unlock, unlearn, and unleash your inner self through Awareness, Acceptance, Trust, Vulnerability, Self-Appreciation, and Inner Child work. Brought to you by Sher Unbound, an Un-Coach who is a lifetime survivor of sexual and domestic violence. Sher is a writer, former Social Worker, Sexual and Domestic Violence Advocate, Family Support Worker, Former Executive Director of a Family Mental Wellness Organization, Tailor, Mother, Grandmother, Explorer, Public Figure, and Influencer living life on her terms. Sher is passionate about women embracing their healthy sensual self and has helped women reclaim their voices and power after sexual and domestic violence. Besides her college education in Counseling and Social Work, Sher's experience and primary education is the school of life. Her chosen coaching team is a close inner circle of trusted philosophers, scholars, and friends, several of whom are also professionals in the Coaching and Educational fields.

Made in the USA
Monee, IL
10 May 2021

68246679R00134